The Camaro in the Pasture

THE 〜〜〜〜〜〜〜〜〜
CAMARO
〜〜〜〜 IN THE
PASTURE

Speculations on the Cultural
Landscape of America

Robert B. Riley

University of Virginia Press

Charlottesville & London

University of Virginia Press
© 2015 by the Rector and Visitors of the University of Virginia
All rights reserved
Printed in the United States of America on acid-free paper

First published 2015

First paperback edition published 2016
ISBN 978-0-8139-3807-3

9 8 7 6 5 4 3 2 1

Library of Congress Cataloging-in-Publication Data is available
from the Library of Congress.

In memory of Brinck

I might not know who I am
but I know where I am from.

—Wallace Stegner

CONTENTS

ACKNOWLEDGMENTS

Even the quickest scanning of this book makes my debt to J. B. Jackson obvious. If I had not known Brinck I certainly would have been doing something else for these many decades, although I am not sure what. That said, these essays still cover more than five decades of writing and this is my one opportunity to acknowledge and thank those many other people who helped me, in many different ways, throughout the years.

As an undergraduate I was fortunate to be a student of David Riesmann, Martin Myerson, and Kevin Lynch, who introduced me to the social, economic, and perceptual aspects of landscape and buildings. As an academic, I have been a colleague of Terry Harkness, who loves the landscape of the Midwest so much, and of John Jakle, who knows so damnably much about it, along with Sue Weideman and Lewis Hopkins, with whom I have shared so many rides through that landscape. I have learned about the cultural landscape from Peirce Lewis, Wilber Zelinsky, Grady Clay, and the most erudite of scholars, Yi-Fu Tuan. I have spent countless hours, and more than a few late nights, in animated, sometimes heated, encounters with Kenny Helphand, Achva Stein, Erv Zube, Catherine Howett, Carl Steinitz, Elen Deming, and Karen Madsen. I have shared many like hours with my environmental design research colleagues: Irv Altman, Sandy Howell, Mike Brill, Setha Low, Clare Cooper Marcus, Amos Rapoport, Perla Korasec, and Nora Rubinstein. My career as a practitioner ended a long time ago, but I still think like a designer, a persistence reinforced by my encounters over the years with the passion, intensity, and energy of Alfred Caldwell, Garrett Eckbo, Peter Walker, Bernard Lassus, and Michael Van Valkenburgh. Thanks to the late Natalie Alpert: critic, guardian, and friend. As I was fortunate in my teachers I have been fortunate in my students, so many of whom have gone on to be respected colleagues, eminent scholars, and talented practitioners. Some have taught me maybe more than they learned from me. It would be a futile attempt to list even a few of them, so as both surrogate and paragon, thanks to Rachel Leibowitz, so long a special person in my personal and professional life. At the University of Virginia Press thanks to Ellen Satrom, who eased my way through the process and procedures of production; to Ruth Melville, the most diligent and resourceful copy editor I have ever encountered; and to Boyd Zenner, insightful and merciless editor, who first conceived this book, but who is liable for none of its shortcomings. Thank you, Brenda Brown, for your friendship, criticism, intellect, high standards, and support for over a quarter of a century. Finally, for Rebeccah, Kimber, and Sarah, who if skeptical, managed to conceal it.

My thanks to the editors of the journals listed below for permission to reprint the following previously published pieces here: "On the Value of the Vernacular: Some Skeptical Thoughts"—*CELA [Council of Educators in Landscape Architecture] Forum* 1, no. 1 (1981); "Autoterritoriality"—*Landscape* 7, no. 3 (1958); "Understanding the Strip"—*Architectural and Engineering News* January 1968; "The Urban Cosmeticians: Or, The City Beautiful Rides Again"—*Landscape* 15, no. 3 (Spring 1966); "The Search for Certainty"—*Arts and Architecture* May 1966; "Green Chaos"—*Harvard Design Magazine* Spring 1997; "What History Should We Teach and Why?"—*Landscape Journal* 14, no. 2 (Fall 1995): 220-25, © 1995 by the Board of Regents of the University of Wisconsin System, reproduced courtesy of the University of Wisconsin Press; "Dreams of Tomorrow"—*Architectural Forum* April 1967; "Reflections on the Landscapes of Memory"—*Landscape* 23, no. 2 (1979); "From Sacred Grove to Disney World: The Search for Garden Meaning"—*Landscape Journal* 7, no. 2 (Fall 1998): 136-47, © 1998 by the Board of Regents of the University of Wisconsin System, reproduced courtesy of the University of Wisconsin Press; "On Criticism"—*Land Forum* 2 (1998); "Some Thoughts on Scholarship and Publication"—*Landscape Journal* 9, no. 1 (Spring 1990): 47-50, © 1990 by the Board of Regents of the University of Wisconsin System, reproduced courtesy of the University of Wisconsin Press; "Speculations on the New American Landscapes"—*Landscape* 24, no. 3 (1980).

The Camaro in the Pasture

♦ ♦ ♦ ♦ Openings

I grew up very much an urban person. I never lived in a city with fewer than two million people, or in a single-family American house, until I was forty years old. "Landscape" was simply what we passed through on vacation or on the way to grandparents' domains, the one of white clapboard houses in a small corn-country town, the other a Victorian extravaganza overlooking the Connecticut River in a now derelict Vermont mill and railroad town. My first college curriculum had no texts, only readings from the "great books," Mortimer Adler's canon from Plato to Freud to Einstein. Then came the contrast of architectural school. One day, in the early 1960s, by now a practicing architect, I was idly browsing through a library and came across, shelved next to one another, copies of J. B. Jackson's journal *Landscape* and *Reading the Landscape* by May Watts. I had never read anything like these books, nor had I ever thought about the things they looked at, nor how they saw them.

Those were heady days for thinking about the environment, about people and our landscape, long, long before the first Earth Day. In a span of just over a year in the early 1960s, four books appeared that changed our way of looking and thinking about the land around us: Jane Jacobs's *The Death and Life of Great American Cities,* Harry Caudill's *Night Comes to the Cumberlands,* Rachel Carson's *Silent Spring,* and Michael Harrington's *The Other America.* Soon after, the untidy and ordinary landscape ("blighted" was then the approved term) came alive for me on a long-distance drive featuring family, pets, and a furniture-laden trailer behind an underpowered van, at the end of a long, long day. After dark off to the left were the lights of Amarillo. What an archetype of the strip's golden age. The motels, the bright lights, the bars, the barbecue restaurants, were more welcome than the proverbial haven of cottage and fireplace on a cold winter night.

Five decades have passed since those books and that trip. Five decades of curiosity, that curiosity I first found in Jackson and Watts. It has been an intellectual treat, the lows of ignorance alternating with the highs of insight. Maybe such an intense intellectual fascination with the landscape is a natural companion to an emotional relation with it.

These essays cover a period of almost exactly fifty years. Some have been published, some not. The first several here are the earliest; beyond that there is only a rough chronological sequence. I have not revised any of these articles, regardless of when they were written, to reflect later conditions, contemporary orthodoxies, or my own hindsights. I have resisted organizing the book into sections, because it was neither written nor conceived that way. I have added a reprise or the briefest of notes to some few where I thought it appropriate.

I am too close to this work, still, to read or feel any consistent themes. Maybe readers will. But in my own mind, there are, if no large themes, at least two constants: a curiosity about how the landscape became what it is and how it is used, and disdain for the silly rhetoric of designers and their pretentions. That might well be the ultimate clash between my two different long-ago schoolings, between the creative and the critical. Not a new story, that.

⫶ On the Value of the Vernacular: Some Skeptical Thoughts

"A landscape architect looking at drive-ins (tractor tire gardens/ local farmsteads/trailer courts/the strip)? Good! It's time someone did something about those eyesores. I cringe every time I drive down Pleasant Valley Road."

"I'm not trying to beautify them. Actually I think we have something to learn from them."

"Learn? What could you possibly learn from them?"

Good question. The interest of the designer in the vernacular landscape is not that of the hobbyist, or the local antiquarian, or the historical geographer. The designer alone seeks lessons applicable to the design process. Fair enough, but what are those lessons? What can the designer really gain from studying the vernacular?

We use the terms "vernacular" and "vernacular landscape" loosely, but with a fair degree of consensus. The word vernacular originally referred to "the native or indigenous language of a country or district." By the mid-nineteenth century, the meaning had been extended to include buildings. Currently it seems to include all widespread buildings or landscape developments not designed by professionals, and even mass-built, professionally designed solutions of design types, like mobile homes and gasoline stations, not traditionally considered the province of the professional designer. As we now seem to use the term, both peasant huts and drive-ins are vernacular, and the term must mean something like "widespread building or landscape solutions that have popular acceptance but are ignored or denigrated by the professional establishment of practitioners and educators." Such a definition is cumbersome but usable and even useful. It also raises some particular problems.

The historical architectural literature, richer in reference to the vernacular than that of landscape architecture, indicates that architects have found at least four uses for the vernacular. They have used formal elements from the vernacular in new buildings, in an effort to make them "fit in." They have seen the vernacular as a source of formal visual inspiration per se, as in Corbusier's rhapsodies on the sculptural massing of grain elevators. They have used it as a philosophical justification for the "rightness" of a particular style—Corbusier on grain elevators again, or the centuries-long romance with the primitive hut documented by Joseph Rykwert. Lastly, they have turned to the vernacular for knowledge about how people interact with the environment—seeking in it clues as to what satisfactions people seek from the designed environment and how they achieve them. This belief seems to dominate, if only implicitly, most serious study of the vernacular by contemporary architects and landscape architects: the hope that the supposedly simpler and more direct processes of vernacular culture and design will provide lessons that will help us to become better designers in our own time and culture.

That hope rests upon several assumptions that are seldom made explicit and almost never examined. Let me mention four.

First is the assumption that the ordinary landscape offers not only knowledge of overall social constraints and process but positive design lessons. The strip, in this view, is worth studying not only because it is a logical response to factors of corporate financing, zoning, land development economics, and automobile use that also affect professionally designed landscapes but also because people find in it solutions and satisfactions similar to those they seek, often in vain, in the professionally designed environment.

Second is the assumption that lessons about design and behavior drawn from other times and cultures, or subcultures, are immediately usable in our own society. Most students of the vernacular, faced with such a bald statement, would probably say, "Oh, of course not, but still . . ." Well, maybe we don't believe it, but we operate as if we did.

Third is the belief that behavior in "primitive" cultures is somehow closer to "real" (or "basic" or "innate" or "natural") behavior than that in more "sophisticated" cultures. Vernacular design solutions are thought to offer us clearer evidence of human response to the environment than those design traditions cluttered up by the meddlesome vanity of priests, kings, or landscape architects.

Fourth is the assumption that the relation between elite and nonelite design traditions is basically the same across cultures or epochs, and that there is more cultural differentiation among elite traditions or designs than among humbler ones. This produces a tendency to see among vernacular traditions similarities or universals that would seem ridiculous if applied to corresponding grand traditions. An example is the currently fashionable idea that the sacred symbols of a tribal society, the wall paintings of a peasant culture, and the pink flamingoes on a subdivision lawn are somehow analogous. Associated with this contention is the belief that design is a symbol-making, or at least symbol-transmitting, activity, and that while current professional design either ignores symbolism or espouses empty or dangerous symbols, vernacular design, in contrast, displays and uses meaningful symbols. Thus, while classic modern architects tried to create symbols for our society (the deification of technology in the work of Mies van der Rohe, for example) and failed, postmodern architects have adopted as symbols certain elements of nonelite culture, such as the gilded TV antenna atop the old folks' home.

These assumptions are naive. The myth of the noble savage, red man or redneck, dies hard. It achieves renewed currency through translation into the currently fashionable academic vocabulary. Given our inadequate knowledge of human behavior and history, few of these assumptions can be completely rejected, any more than they can be validated. It is imperative, however, to recognize that many of our claims for study of the value of the vernacular are based upon certain assumptions and that these assumptions are open to serious question.

A common feature of these assumptions is the lumping together of what might more productively be considered distinct phenomena. This is true, for example, of the definition of vernacular offered earlier, which says more about what vernacular is not than what it is. We could attempt a more precise definition of the term—in the process disqualifying some buildings or landscapes now included—but this seems neither necessary nor productive. What is necessary is recognition of the diversity of buildings, landscapes, and cultures commonly included under the term vernacular, and a great caution in drawing analogies or eliciting universals from among them. What might be productive is the development of more precise categories within that broad class of vernacular.

Consider, as an example, "vernacular" domestic ornament and its symbolism. While there might indeed be parallels between African wall decorations and the wagon wheels on suburban lawns, there is more to be learned from such ornaments, and their role in a culture and their relation to the task of design, by studying their similarities and differences than by baldly lumping them together in a grand polemic.

I suggest a crude and preliminary alternative—a view of domestic symbolic ornament that recognizes three types lying on a continuum.

1. Sacred ornament symbolic of the supernatural or the cosmos. This is characterized by rigidly determined elements, with form and meaning evolving very slowly if at all, and the freedom of the individual artisan or possessor to modify the form extremely limited.

2. "Peasant" (for want of a better term) ornament. Form and meaning might derive from type 1, but here sacred determinants are minor in comparison to the above. Strong cultural constraints exist as to placement, form, and material, but within them considerable individual creative variation is permitted, or even emphasized. This type displays the designer-cherished theme of variety within order; a visual order at the larger scale is thought to visually unify a settlement, while variety at a smaller scale offers interest and individuality. Wall incisions and paintings on African dwellings and granaries are a good example.

3. Personalization. Ornament is highly idiosyncratic, exhibiting no obvious cultural unity in either form or meaning. At one extreme, it is as

imaginative as the Watts Towers; at the other it descends to garden kitsch. Sometimes it is simply the placement of purchased, mass-produced items.

Note that none of these categories require distinguishing ornament designed or made by the owner or user from that designed or made by others, an easy dichotomy that proves of surprisingly little value for classifying vernacular ornament.

These categories make sense to me as a designer; they seem at least acceptable anthropologically. They raise obvious questions. Are they exclusive, or can they coexist within a given culture? Are they tied to any broad characterizations of cultural types, such as primitive, peasant, and industrial society? Are there recurring relationships between the themes and forms of residential ornament and other aspects of a culture, such as kinship systems or food-producing technology or settlement patterns? What happens to ornamentation when a culture undergoes industrialization? Many other questions arise. If they are not questions that designers can answer, they are questions that designers should consider before producing manifestos on the value of the vernacular.

Let me suggest two other areas in which it seems imperative to begin drawing distinctions. The first is in the characterization, or lack thereof, of cultural types. The development of cultural typologies has passed out of fashion in anthropology, but surely it remains the province of that discipline. Designers should be wary of bandying about simplistic cultural categories no longer considered tenable, let alone productive, by anthropologists; they should be even warier of lumping all "non-grand" design traditions together. Lack of such care has led to a dangerous fallacy common to much current discussion on the vernacular—the confusion of folk culture and products with the popular culture and products of an industrialized, media-dominated society . . . the equation of an eighteenth-century cottage with a split-level ranchette or of a millet bin with a grain elevator. Robert Redfield's distinction between the great tradition and the little tradition is stimulating and productive for students of buildings and landscapes, but the seductive temptation to apply it to contemporary American culture should be resisted. More useful is Henry Glassie's distinction between three types of culture—elite, folk, and mass or popular. He sees folk culture as standing in sharp contrast to popular culture. The former is relatively stable, draws its inspiration from tradition, and can best be classified by geographical region; the latter changes rapidly, draws its inspiration from the media, and is best classified by time period. Folk buildings and gardens do evolve over time, thereby providing material for doctoral dissertations, but they do so slowly, by contiguous diffusion or through population migration. Drive-in styles change quickly, and leap from one region to a distant one by corporate fiat. Glassie sees more similarity between elite and popular culture than between folk and popular culture, and surely the architecture of the strip is closer to that of the practicing establishment tradition than it is to a peasant dwelling of the little tradition.

Secondly, a distinction must be made between style, in the sense of a viable building or landscape tradition, and fashion. It is not easy to define precisely either term, or the difference between them, but there remains a difference that must be recognized. Sigfried Giedion distinguished between transitory and constituent facts. Alfred Kroeber saw fashions as transient nodes overlying style. George Kubler viewed styles as occupying an intermediary position between tools and fashions and perhaps summed up the essence of the difference: that styles can be developed but fashions only copied. That a building or landscape phenomenon is rejected or ignored in traditional practice or education is not a guarantee of its viability or value. To see every popular landscape fad as "honest vernacular idiom" is silly, sloppy, and an evasion of moral responsibility.

These contentions might seem negative and ill tempered, but they are the troubled thoughts of someone who has spent a long time looking at common buildings and landscapes, admiring them, and wondering about their meaning. The study of vernacular buildings and landscapes is valuable, in many ways: for visual inspiration, for getting away from desk or drawing board and onto the road, for writing off vacations as tax deductions, for forming societies and taking all-night diner tours, for getting grants for boarding the historic preservation bandwagon, and for justifying new courses. It might even turn out to tell us more about what people seek in their environment, and make us more responsible designers. But above all, it is valuable in itself, as a knowledge-seeking, curiosity-arousing demonstration of the incredible complexity, variety, and ingenuity of human culture and design. It would be a shame if, inflated by pretentious claims, it were to become merely another academic fashion, destined to pass as quickly as the golden arches of not so long ago.

◢ ◢ ◢ ◢ Autoterritoriality

Strange how little thought has been given to the behavioral implications of the automobile. The planners' dislike of the ever-accelerating American dependence on the automobile is a major determinant of much contemporary urban design discussion. Unrestricted use of the private car has its disadvantages. It pollutes. It is an inefficient method of peak-load transportation to and from the crowded centers of our cities. It demands heavy expenditures in the public sector and, proportionately, perhaps even higher private expenditures for the two-car commuter family. It magnifies the already difficult problem of preserving wilderness areas. Most seriously of all, it is producing a new city shape that the planning profession, educated in traditional concepts of urban physical structure, has so far been unable to cope with.

But the anti-automobile bias of the professionals seems to be based upon more than such rational objections. Putting aside supercilious descriptions of the American's car as a love-image or a totem, the fact remains that the automobile does have a meaning that for many people reaches far beyond its function—an emotional attachment represented by the weekend rituals of washing or tinkering. It might be just this attachment, as much as functional limitation, which explains the planners' low opinion of the private car. Somehow, strolling the streets, sipping wine at a sidewalk cafe, playing chess in the park, sampling the art galleries, or even gathering for darts at a pub are all considered worthwhile pastimes for the urban dweller, while repairing or grooming cars is somehow distasteful. This is a distinction that smacks at bottom of class consciousness or snobbery. It is a reflection of the profession's unspoken vision of the city as primarily a stimulating setting for the urbane connoisseur.

But far more dangerous than the planners' emotional aversion to the automobile is their total failure to understand the reasons for its popularity. The kind of pseudo-Freudian analysis popularized by John Keats and others is more useful in justifying existing prejudices than in furthering real understanding. And yet in the collection of contemporary planning concepts there exists a powerful and obvious tool for understanding the automobile's role—the concept of territoriality.

There is more than a bit of gobbledygook, silliness, and plain misunderstanding in the designers' current preoccupation with some of the newer concepts of the psychology of spatial perception. But the work of Edward Hall and others has shown, plainly and surely, that men move through, build around them, and carry about with them certain structured volumes of psychologically differentiated space. There is doubt as to how these spatial volumes are best understood, and doubt as to their exact meaning, but there should be no doubt as to their existence or their importance in certain settings. Nor should there be doubt that constriction or expansion of these distinct spaces, or conflicts between them, or ambiguities as to their boundaries, can cause uncertainty and stress.

This idea of people living within a range of simultaneous spatial domains, graded from the intimately personal to the plainly public, should explain, more satisfactorily than any of the familiar psychiatric or sociological clichés, the attraction of the automobile. Put simply, the automobile allows one to travel almost at will anywhere in the public domain while remaining in a completely private world unequivocally defined by physical boundaries. The maintenance, defense, or even definition of this intensely personal space no longer needs to be achieved by psychological adaptation or cultural understanding or ritual. It is marked off structurally—with clarity and solidity. Maybe Americans are more concerned than most peoples with the definition of personal space, though Hall claims that the Germans are even more jealous of its boundaries. It might be that the rapid and continuing changes in the American social scene over the last fifty years have produced a general uncertainty and unease that places more importance and value upon the protection and clear definition of the private personal realm. While the traditional utopian visions have been built around a communal structure, modern Americans are attempting to build very personal or at least familial utopias—utopias structured around detached houses, television, and automobiles. There is at any rate a basic distinction between the automobile and other methods of transportation that far transcends convenience and economy, a distinction that must be understood. It is the distinction between public and private transportation, not in the sense of financing or titular ownership or even trip scheduling, but in the sense of the personal perception of space patterns.

This ability to move through public space without suffering impingements upon, or readjustment of, one's own personal space could explain much more than the commuter's attachment to his private automobile. It might partly explain the phenomenal success of the auto rental companies, for a rental car allows one to travel a strange and foreign and often confusing public world in a kind of instant privacy and encapsulated security. It might partly explain, as much as laziness, the propensity for taking automobiles into "wilderness" areas—areas that by definition lie at the opposite extreme from personalized space. Surely it explains much of the success of the motel business, for a motel is more than just convenient—it enables one to move between the personal spaces of car and bedroom without traveling through the more public and often spatially ambiguous realms of lobby, elevator, and corridor associated with the traditional hotel.

It must be understood that the automobile is not just a more or less efficient competitor of public transit, nor must the emotional importance of the automobile be contemptuously dismissed as some psychological aberration. It might be that in certain parts of our older cities the side effects of the private automobile are so space and time consuming, so physically wasteful or even unhealthy, as to require restrictions on its use. It might be that the only way of increasing the acceptance of "public" transportation is to incorporate into it as much of the spatial quality of the automobile as is possible. But the transportation problems of our urban regions are not going to be solved until we admit to an understanding of the very special spatial features of the automobile. The appeal of the automobile is not just a silly habit easily gotten rid of, but a means of satisfying a deeply human territoriality.

♦ ♦ ♦ ♦ Understanding the Strip

The strip is a land of pop architecture . . .

It is a land of neon and autos, of open space and bizarre architecture, of used-car lots and discount stores. It comes alive in the afternoon and stays alive most of the night, perhaps all night. It might be the extended main street of a small town, the access road for a freeway or a suburb, or the dominating element of a new western metropolis of several hundred thousand people. It is exuberant and tacky. Its visual impact seems endless in front and behind, but ends abruptly a few yards to right or left. Wherever it is, it is where the action is. Its name is the strip—and planners wish that it would go away.

The strip is not easy to define in conventional architectural or planning terms. It is as much a symbol as it is a physical thing. But if its definition is vague, its image is clear enough—a garish neon wilderness of tourist traps and shoddy used-car lots, an ugly and disreputable blot on the landscape. The image is vivid—and suspect.

Two things should be made clear about the strip. First of all, despite its motels, it is not primarily oriented toward the tourist. The vast majority of its businesses are identical to the ones found downtown or in any neighborhood commercial area or any new shopping center. Its motels are the meeting places of local civic clubs, its drive-ins the congregating places of local teenagers. Secondly, it happens to be much more important than we care to admit. It is commonly the activity center for the urban fringes and the suburban area beyond. Like it or not, it is in many cases far more successful than downtown and just as prosperous as the elaborate new shopping centers with their pedestrian malls. It is a healthy response to new patterns of living, and it is not going to go away.

What the strip needs most is understanding and direction. Its importance in the lives of many people demands that planners stop condemning it and begin facing it. Before we can worry about how it looks, however, we need to know how it works. Why are some strips successful and others not? Why, on a particular street, do some stretches prosper, while others a few blocks away languish and die? While a large body of economic lore has been compiled for shopping centers, very little is known about the economics of strip development. Indeed, much of the blighted appearance associated with the strip is a result not of poor taste but of economic failure—ranks of empty stores and abandoned signs standing as proof that businessmen, investors, and lenders understand little more of the strip than do planners.

Amid the general ignorance, though, one fact is clear. Much of the strip's blight is due not to the fact of strip zoning, but to an overabundance of it, a fulfillment of the idea that every important traffic carrier should have its chance at becoming a major commercial area. The result is a distorted set of land values and patchwork patterns of open land that follow no rules of the marketplace—a chaos that is economic as well as visual. The first step in setting up the strip as a healthy working enterprise is the restriction of strip commercial zoning.

Such a restriction, however, is only a first step in organization. We must also understand how neighboring uses and circulation affect the economics of the strip. What parts do the quality, proximity, and economic level of neighboring residential areas play? Do large shopping centers nearby help or hinder strip businesses? How do the number and traffic capacity of cross streets affect the strip? Is it more successful if feeder streets terminate at it, or continue across it? How do nearby freeway interchanges influence its economic potential? We know little about how businesses affect one another. Are there key businesses that radiate a field of better economic potential, key businesses comparable to department stores in large shopping centers? Does a concentration of diverse stores attract more people? If one must leave a parking lot and reenter traffic to visit the next store, does it matter whether it be for a block or a mile? What factors most affect consumer preferences—distance, ease of parking, check-cashing facilities, drive-in windows, or personal buyer-seller relations?

Answers to these questions are not going to produce some drastic restructuring of what we see around us. The strip is not a shopping center; one of its attractions is the fact that within economic limitations a businessman can do pretty much as he pleases with his property. But some thought on these questions might well lead to more careful planning by individual entrepreneurs, resulting at least in a more healthy strip, if not yet a better-looking one.

Is Neon Ugly?

If no one knows anything about the economics of the strip, everyone knows all about its visual qualities—ghastly! The American Institute of Architects' anti-ugliness campaign features it as the prosecution's exhibit number one; "doing something about that horrible neon" ranks just behind the magic phrase "urban renewal" in the target priority list of enlightened civic groups.

But in the last decade it has become fashionable for designers to praise Times Square and Piccadilly Circus for the exciting qualities of their disorganized neon hodge-podge. Is it unreasonable to ask that we be equally ready to accept the strip for what it is? The visual effect of the strip can be much improved, but only if we work with what it has to offer.

It is by nature a place where buildings are small, or at least low, and unrelated to the street; where signs are visually more important than the structures they advertise; where "space leaks out," not because of careless design, but because of the need for parking and off-street automobile circulation; where a mixture of shopping and through transit precludes either the grand scale of the freeway or the solid enclosure of an older business street. We are not going to improve it by tidying it up or by trying to turn it into something that it is not and never will be.

There are things we can do about it. First among these is to tie it into its surroundings. One of the major visual failings of the strip is that it is unrelated to what goes on alongside it—even if one knows where one is on the strip, one is unlikely to know where one is in the city. This needed visual identification could be provided by clear and studied treatment of the major grid streets crossing the strip. Such crossings are places for high buildings, contrasting uses, or intense greenery. One could then tie the strip to the city by recognizing major intersections as keys to the important streets serving the adjacent areas.

Jostling Helps

We can improve the strip by concentrating the commercial activity along it. The strip is most exciting and alive where its signs and businesses jostle each other side by side, clamoring for attention; most depressing where a few scattered signs and stores pop up, one or two a block.

Economics makes it unlikely that commercial uses will cluster together of their own free will, but other uses could be introduced onto vacant land. Contemporary planning dogma decrees the mixing of institutional, commercial, and recreational uses downtown. Is there any reason, apart from prejudice, why the same philosophy should not be applied to the strip, already the activity center for many communities? Enough land so used would lead to more intense development in the remaining commercial areas.

The introduction of diverse uses would serve to remedy another of the strip's faults—its monotony. Even if we were able to line the strip with solid neon, several unrelieved miles of it might be too much of a good thing. The strip badly needs a clearer organization within itself.

It needs a beginning, it needs an end, and it needs articulation of its own diverse elements. Knowing where the strip is within the city is not enough; one should also have visual pegs along the road itself. If we assume that the spatial character and composition of the present small businesses along the road are a reasonably logical response to strip economics, a development that cannot be changed without serious damage, then clearly the key to visual organization lies in the well-chosen insertion of other elements: large-scale buildings for varied uses.

No Need for Uniformity

No matter how uniform any strip might look at first, it likely contains a potential framework for subdivision and internal definition, a framework made in large part from elements independent of existing development. The rhythm of regularly spaced major cross arteries is one such element. Visual barriers such as highway and railroad overpasses, or nodes such as freeway interchanges, are others. Natural features such as water crossings, hills, and remaining stands of thick trees possess an organizing potential, as do the subtle directional shifts in the road itself, shifts now too often camouflaged by the buildings.

Beyond these inherent possibilities for definition, the insertion of diverse uses would allow the planner to establish stretches of contrasting visual character. Schools could be placed as walls along the road, giving that rare strip experience, a sense of enclosure, or planned as large, walled open spaces perpendicular to the road, providing a strong cross axis. Parks offer the same opportunity, a generous cross axis or a solid enclosing wall of green parallel to the road. Long buildings, medium high (seven or eight stories would do the job), can furnish transverse visual barriers, and tall point blocks provide points of emphasis.

The essential trick of visual organization is simply to mix in small areas of different character carefully placed to emphasize existing natural rhythms. Point blocks, for example, could mark changes in road direction; walls of buildings or greenery could extend solidly between existing visual barriers, or from one major intersection to the next. The result could be not one long weak and uniform sensation, but a sequence of varied experiences.

Accepting the Strip

The strip could be a satisfying a coherent urban element. To accomplish this, we must first stop damning it. Why not accept it as a natural and successful response to new living patterns?

Then we must try to understand how it works. If we can do these things, we can also make it a meaningful visual experience. This neither a matter of superficial tidying up nor of radical reorganization but one of supplying certain elements in the right places and leaving the rest to develop as it has and will.

This will require patience, care, and a level of planning far above what now exists. Renewing a decaying downtown is not easy either, but many cities are attempting this. To many Americans today, the strip is as important as downtown was in its prime. It deserves the same respect.

Reprise

The Las Vegas we "learned from," Jackson's western cruising strip, and American graffiti are not as we remember them. It is ironic that Vegas and Jackson's strip were lumped together, conflation causing confusion, when they were different in so many ways. There were commonalities: freestanding buildings clamoring for attention through over-the-top signage and Googie architecture completely serving the automobile . . . the resemblance ended there. Vegas was what was later defined as a "destination resort," dominated by outside big money and big consumer spending: the other was a purely local phenomenon, marginal enterprises catering to casual local traffic. But in fact there were, and are, many different kinds of strips. Grady Clay once analyzed some of these, but slotted them in a developmental progression that was perhaps more conceptual than on-the-ground real. Some reminders and remnants of that prototypical strip survive, but more important is our cultural memory, the strip as symbol of the high times and easy living of the 1950s, right down through occasional newly built retro-Googie burger stands. Look up "Woodwarding" in a search engine and you will find most of the references center on nostalgia. In Vegas the decorated sheds and mega ducks have yielded to the world's largest collection of designer-controlled, encapsulated environments, the fantasyland for half the world.

Probably the first change in Jackson's strip came as national franchises increasingly replaced local businesses. The larger motels became local meeting places for business organizations and miniconventions. As the dominance of national operations increased, gaudy signs and bizarre building shapes became less important. New enterprises began to rely less on elaborate individual signage than on symbols and icons recognizable from national advertising and television. Kent Macdonald neatly called this new version "television road." The latest revision to my local McDonald's sports only one very shallow, yellow, pasteboard-looking arc slapped directly onto the building's front (i.e., the side that faces the street but of course has no entrance). Next came a remarkable change of scale as the "big boxes" proliferated and in their totality formed a "mega strip." The big boxes sit far back from the road, with maybe some tiny conifers dotted tastefully along the right-of-way. Instead of roadside signage, simple lettering modest in design but huge in scale spreads across the fronts of the buildings.

But the current big-box mega strip is in turn transforming into a different spatial organization, the whole as much transverse as linear. To abstract it, forget that ribbon of large beads and picture instead a branching tree. The new form, which we might call the *compound strip,* has major cross axes with buildings fronting onto them as well. But beyond, in an area that might best be called "behind the boxes," there is a myriad of small linear buildings, each housing four to eight modest businesses. This is the low-rent district of the compound strip: electronic gaming stores, cell phone brokers, dry cleaners, and the like. The space is cheap, flexible, and transient, one business replacing another regularly. These are the kind of low-end ventures found long ago on the cheaper parts of Colfax Avenue in Denver, Central Avenue in Albuquerque, or Speedway in Tucson, but with pawnshops replaced by quick-turnover payday loan operations, not lined up along a road but thrown down around small parking spaces, with no pretense of even token plantings.

It is tempting to think of this form as an exploded suburban shopping mall dispersed haphazardly. But the compound strip accommodates cheaper operations that could not survive in the mall. Think instead of the traditional downtown business district sliced into one-story increments, maybe further sectioned, each split up in and scattered around almost haphazardly in a financial pecking order. I think of the Loop in Chicago when I was young. There the major department stores, like today's big boxes, were arranged linearly, mostly along State Street. But in between these major players were nondescript midrise business buildings, populated at the top end by dentists and perhaps law offices, at the lower end by leather repair services, button shops, and cut-rate furriers.

This is not the old strip, nor just the mega strip, but a new complex shopping arrangement. Just as "the strip" came to be termed "strip commercial," this form might still carry an image of strip, but the reality is more complex. It is the ultimate expression of today's commerce. It serves well as a business area. What has gone, probably forever, is any sense of casual community. Even in the shopping malls there was communal, if temporary and transient, space where one could sit and just watch. The old Courthouse Square populated only by strangers? This is no space here for the flaneur.

At the other end of the scale, the familiar old mini strip mall is back, in a resurgence featuring not pawnshops, nor marginal hobby stores, nor used booksellers, but more upscale enterprises. Here you find solo practice doctors, specialty food shops, wine purveyors, high fashion–aping clothing and furniture boutiques, a small coffee shop, and a laser surgery operation that never seems to be open. Gentrified architecture here means token dwarf conifer plantings, a continuous arcade, two-dimensional plywood gables, plaster columns, and apparently a rental scale that dooms the affluent amateurs and results in a high turnover. And where is all the neon, those flashing arrows, those tilted martini glasses? Gone along with the flaneur.

↲ ↲ ↲ ↲ The Urban Cosmeticians:
Or, The City Beautiful Rides Again

The American Institute of Architects is leading us, it boasts, to war—a community war against ugliness. And as with most wars there are catchy slogans and fighting phrases aplenty, but little serious discussion of the financial costs or the strategic realities, and even less questioning as to whether this war is really necessary. Along with the usual displays, mailings, and films, the AIA has also produced what might be called a manual of war: Paul Spreiregen's *Urban Design: The Architecture of Towns and Cities*, a book that makes clear not only the objectives, strategy, and tactics of the campaign but its limitations as well.

Urban Design is a popularized introduction—a book meant not for the professional city planner or pioneering architect but for the student or average architect or interested layman. It is analogous—and not in a derogatory sense—to a weekend artist's guide to oil painting, or an introduction to interior decorating. It is an attempt both to explain urban design and to arouse enthusiasm for it. It covers the same categories as such guides: a history of the art, an introduction to principles of beauty, a survey of materials and techniques, a step-by-step guide on how to start, and even a survey of where to go for money and equipment. It is written plainly and simply, if not stylishly, and covers its material as thoroughly as any introductory survey could. But the fault of the book, and of the whole AIA campaign, is that it substitutes enthusiasm for thoughtful consideration of goals.

It is not easy to quarrel with a war against ugliness. Beauty is a fine thing. But many futile and ultimately sordid wars have been fought for high principles. Before going off to enlist, it would be well to ask whether the war can be won and whether it is, ultimately, a war worth winning.

The AIA has by now told us pretty clearly what urban design, or civic beauty, is. It has told us very little about how to achieve it in the face of long-standing and widespread lack of interest. We are not a country of simple people doing simple things carefully in traditional and honored ways—the surest way to create beauty. Neither are we a country where an elite minority can impose its ideals upon a society—the way in which the traditionally beautiful cities of history have been achieved. We are a country with a historical and contemporary disregard for beauty. Other things—speculative profit, an arms race, a space race, or a cure for cancer—have been and are more important to us. Neither the AIA war against ugliness nor its cousin, the National Highway Beautification campaign, has ever faced this fact, at least publicly, perhaps for fear of offending the very people whom they must win over as generals and soldiers. But the White House, in its beautification campaign, at least offers some idea of how to begin. The idea seems to be to get people to care, both pressure groups and the general unorganized public. This is to be done not only through high-sounding conferences and seminars but through pronouncements from high people in high places, political pressure, and unashamed advertising. The AIA, though, guarding the architect's image as a "professional man" and at the same time ballyhooing him as the master purveyor of comprehensive services—the creator and savior of urban beauty—is confining itself to the institutional soft sell. The politicians, as usual, are much more realistic. For if, as seems likely, the only way to have "beauty" in this land is to create a consumer desire for it, then the thing to do is pull out all the stops and let Madison Avenue have at it. If we must have beauty, if seminars and after-dinner speakers won't do the trick, then let's have billboards and full-color double-spread ads reading "Help fight urban blight," "Put a painting in your parlor," and "Our region has 43% fewer 'road towns.'" It is easy, of course, to be witty or snide about such ideas, but there remains the problem of how to achieve beauty when few care about it.

The AIA admits that beauty needs planning. Now, public acceptance of planning is a hard thing to come by in this country. Zoning has been accepted and so to a lesser extent has urban renewal. But extrapolating acceptance of these tools into a future acceptance of wider and more restrictive planning is wishful thinking. Both zoning and urban renewal have been accepted largely because they offered to some the opportunity for quick and plentiful profit. But planning cannot be sold on the basis of profit forever. There comes a time when wise planning for the many means financial loss for some, or even for many. When that happens, planners are usually the losers. This is another issue the proponents of total urban design have yet to face.

But the anti-ugliness campaign is questionable not only on the point of whether its goals are realistic. The goals themselves are questionable. To begin with, the ideal of urban beauty held up to us is the city of the past. The anti-ugliness campaign recognizes the forces that have changed the city since the Industrial Revolution: the train, the trolley, the telegraph, the telephone, the turnpike. It recognizes them as forces that structured the city of the last century or more, and proposes to use them as forces to structure planned growth in the future. But if regions are to be shaped by such technological forces, the smaller parts of the city are to remain in essence what they were hundreds of years ago. The architect's mind lies with the automobile, the shopping center, and rapid transit, but his heart lies with Florence, Bloomsbury, and Suzhou. The justification given is that although means of transport change, the measure of the human eye and foot remain constant. With this reasoning, architects and planners are everywhere busy inserting squares and plazas in models of urban redevelopment schemes. It might be wise to ask, though, whether social desires and the sense of scale have not changed too. Will all those little Piazza San Marcos be filled with happy people, shopping, strolling idly, sitting, sipping wine? Or will the people who are presumed to want such spaces continue to spend Saturdays towing a power boat two hundred miles for two hours of speeding around a reservoir?

The AIA approach to urban design may underrate the changes that the Industrial Revolution has produced. The changes that are to come will be even more drastic; they are ignored completely. Our grandchildren or their grandchildren may live in a world where antigravity belts or self-powered mechanically self-sufficient dwelling units will have done away with fixed bed transport and even cities. Architecture might, before too long, be not a matter of fixed, immutable ground-rooted shells but of disposable cell units, or even small climate makers without walls or roofs. The visionary city plans of our times, the "metabolism" cities, the plug-in cities, play no part in the AIA city scheme. The AIA, of course, is planning for today, but a plan for today that ignores tomorrow is a poor plan indeed.

Reprise

Where did that "war on ugliness" go? Into that obscurity to which most such high-minded bluster phrases are doomed, I guess. On the other hand,

"America the Beautiful" seems to have returned whence it came—the local garden club. And as for "urban renewal," has any planning concept descended from an ideal into a pejorative so quickly and completely, today connoting evil as much as "colonialism"? We now have "urban revitalization," which, when it is not stripping less-than-tasteful additions from the fronts of row houses in search of a more moneyed clientele, dresses up our shopping streets. It brings a part-old, part-new physical vocabulary: the eternal bedding plants now sitting in designer boxes; some tastefully minimal sign regulation; street lights reminiscent of the nineteenth century; designer-approved bicycle racks; a variety of paving materials ("hardscape") suggesting bricks and cobblestones, the real materials being too tempting for litigation; and cast-iron grates for the trees, the trees, trees everywhere. How long ago was it that J. B. Jackson noted how Americans idolized trees in their residential districts but thought them unfitting for their business districts? Specimen trees lining boulevards, major urban axes, or shopping streets à la Fifth Avenue are one thing, their proliferation along our ordinary business streets another. How many trees does one find along the ordinary shopping streets of London, Paris, or Rome? Maybe the beautificationists, now apparently friends with city councils and their engineers, have won after all. But might we not be better off putting those trees in municipal parking lots, much more in need of amenities than our business streets?

Justification for this inanely named and often ineptly executed "streetscaping" mania now comes under the general rubric of building, or rebuilding, "a sense of community." That also seems the premise and promise of the "New Urbanism," which of course is neither new nor urban, but an exercise in nostalgia.

Here it comes again, then, the eternal ego-myth that listening to designers, with their cyclically fluctuating peccadillos and predilections, will produce not just a new designer look but richer lives and better-behaved communities for all. Twenty-five years ago we were similarly consumed with closing off those same streets and inserting giant planters. Will we never learn?

◢ ◢ ◢ ◢ The Search for Certainty

The current state of architecture has been persistently described as one of chaos. Now the word "chaos" is significant. Why not "diversity" or even "freedom"? Chaos, diversity, and freedom, respectively, are words of negative, neutral, and positive feeling. The common choice of chaos tells us a great deal not only about contemporary architecture but about our basic beliefs. We face a diversity of style and philosophy and we do not like it. We may accept it as unavoidable but we are uneasy. In our hearts we feel that it is wrong, somehow immoral. Rather than welcoming our uncertainty as a chance for variety and individual expression, we seek to mold from it a common approach, a universal way of working, unique to our time. We seek a style, not in the derogatory sense of the word as applied to nineteenth-century eclecticism, but in the historic sense, as applied to the truly great architectural epochs of the past. Now architects are not so naive as to think that this is their problem alone. They realize that their predicament is a reflection of the confused state of the time. But there persists the feeling that this confusion lies only on the surface, that it can be blamed on the architectural press, on Madison Avenue, or on the abundance of materials and techniques. Underneath, we feel, there is a unity in society, a unity that architecture should express, a unity that can be called the "dominant," our very own Zeitgeist. We hope that through inquiry, discipline, and self-denial we can master the confusion and create the unique architecture that will serve that dominant.

What are the sources of this desire for a unique way of building, this search for certainty? Why do we reject diversity, be it called freedom or chaos? Why is there diversity rather than unity? Is it desirable or even possible to mold a style from this diversity? If it is impossible now, when and under what conditions might it be possible? First of all, we should realize that this desire for discipline is not unique to our time. It has been a recurring theme for over four hundred years. The Renaissance broke forever the chains that had bound the architect. It transformed him from a semianonymous artisan and builder, working within limited unconscious, unexamined cultural goals, into a rational, self-conscious, individual designer. It gave him freedom: a freedom that has caused him pain as well as pleasure—a freedom from which he has periodically fled. When, as in the age of the baroque, society has given the architect strong direction, or when, as in the early twentieth century, strong new philosophies in art have arisen, the architect has responded energetically. But when there has been no strong cultural direction, no exciting artistic ferment, he has not been notably happy with his freedom. Great figures such as Claude-Nicolas Ledoux and Sir John Soane have used such a vacuum to develop powerful individual styles. Most architects, though, have been content to putter aimlessly about and retreat into the nearest stylistic refuge. This retreat has usually led to imitation; to the academy. The rise of mannerism was the first retreat. The bold and confident inventiveness of the Renaissance was replaced by imitation, eclecticism, and a reliance on theory and history. The nineteenth century was another such time, one that produced an unprecedented architectural muddle. That muddle still shapes our thinking.

Society is conservative and slow to accept change in the arts. To overcome this inertia the artist must not only say, "What we offer is better than what we now have," but must add, "What we now have is distasteful, ugly, and untrue." And so the search for a new expression begins with sweeping condemnation of the status quo as immoral. Exposure of the weaknesses and excesses of existing styles is the propaganda by which a new movement seeks acceptance, and the negative features of a style shape the claims made for its successor. The excesses of nineteenth-century architecture were its unrestrained individuality and its historicism, and so the leaders of the modern revolt promised an architecture that was to be supraindividual and unique of its time. But there is a difference between negative aspects of an abandoned style and positive features capable of building a new one. The Victorian failures were so obvious that ever since it has seemed easy to do better. The architects of the last century were conspicuously out of touch with their time. This fact, however, has not made it any easier for us to find a consensus that truly represents our time. But the task still obsesses us. The disastrous failure of the Victorians has left us both with a distorted view of our own purpose and a false confidence in our ability to find a solution for what may still be an insoluble problem.

The failure of the nineteenth century has led to an uncertainty about our role, a self-consciousness that has changed the nature of architectural thinking. The contemporary architect, haunted by the ghost of nineteenth-century eclecticism, faces a dilemma. On the one hand we remember our early promise to achieve a universal and uniquely contemporary way of building. On the other hand we are terrified at the idea of creating a "style" in the nineteenth-century sense. As a result we search for answers lying outside the field of architectural design proper.

> . . . the Modern Architect . . . has, for some reason or another stepped out of his *rôle,* taken a look at the scene around him and then become obsessed with the importance not of architecture, but of the *relation* of architecture to other things. . . . He has . . . left the first personality at the drawing board and taken the second (the "live" personality) on a world-tour of contemporary life—scientific research, sociology, psychology, engineering, the arts and a great many other things. Returning to the drawing board he finds the first personality embarrassing and profoundly unattractive. There he stubbornly sits, smelling slightly of "the styles." So the second personality sits down beside him and painfully guides his hand. . . . he is terrified that . . . if he should concentrate again on the exposition and elaboration of purely architectural values he would commit the terrible sin of creating a "style." Of this possibility he has an unmitigated horror. (John Summerson)

We reject diversity. We seek a consensus, a common approach. But this proposed vocabulary is not to be based upon the "stylistic" preferences of designers. It is to be something bigger, more basic. It must come from the dominant spirit of our time, as surely as did the Doric and the Gothic from theirs.

What we seek is rejection of the entire post-Gothic concept of the architect. Our role as self-conscious individual designers is no longer acceptable to us. Whether this discontent is just a yearning for supposedly "simpler" times (Summerson's "fable of the Golden Age") or a portent of a new postmodern role in a mass society we cannot now tell. We should, however, understand its implications and admit that it is conditioned at least partly by a hangover from the intemperate excesses of the nineteenth century.

But if there are historical reasons for our attitude, there are also powerful forces in contemporary life which strengthen it. We live today in a society where too many things are possible and too few guidelines for choice are available, the only commonly accepted rules those of the price system.

Architects are no more immune to the effects of this situation than anyone else. To fully understand the architectural search for certainty is to see it as part of a general, widespread response to the uncertainties of life today. Erich Fromm has distinguished between "freedom from" and "freedom to" and pointed out that we seek the former and avoid the latter. We seek simple answers and external rules so that we may escape the lonely burden of individual choice. Is it possible that the desire for architectural unity and discipline stems partly from the same fear of uncertainty that has produced the right-wing political reaction of America in the 1960s? We should examine our feelings closely and ask whether we are honestly condemning an unhealthy state of chaos, or retreating from a freedom that has become too much to bear.

That search for a common style must be seen in a larger perspective than that usually comprehended. It must be understood in terms of our reaction to nineteenth-century architecture and our reaction to the awesome freedom of choice of the twentieth century. But although such historical and sociological explanations may help us in understanding our feelings, they do not help us in creating architecture. They do not tell us why diversity exists or whether it is possible or even desirable to end that diversity.

To understand why our time has produced such architectural diversity we must understand three aspects of our culture: its acceleration, its centrifugality, and its self-conscious individuality. We exist in a time of rapidly accelerating change. We are aware of this condition but have not yet faced up to its architectural implications. An example of this blindness is our attitude toward "the decline and fall of the curtain wall." Leaving aside historical quibbling about its intellectual ancestry, we can say that the metal curtain wall as an actual widespread means of building is a style that has bloomed, matured, and decayed in approximately twenty years. This unexpected short life has been an unpleasant surprise for most of us. We have blamed its death on deficiencies in the style itself ("dehumanized boxes") or on a corrupted architectural climate ("architects are just looking for the latest taste thrill"). We have overlooked two important things. Firstly, the metal curtain wall is—or was—a style just as Doric and Gothic were. Like them it was an honest and supraindividual style based on the realities of the time, and it went through the same cycle of birth, maturation, and decay. It died when, and because, it had said everything it had to say. Secondly, its life span was so brief, not because the style was "untrue" nor because taste has been debauched, but because our timescale is radically different. Processes that formerly took two centuries or more now take perhaps one-tenth as long. This is a terribly important fact of life in our age. Our timescale has been drastically changed. We cannot expect any style, no matter how valid, no matter how grand its expression, to live more than a small fraction of the time associated with the great styles of the past.

Our society is diverse and fragmented. Various parts of it have different values and move in different directions. Societies of the past were unified and moved in one direction. Different values and directions may have existed, but only as minor contrapuntal themes woven around one dominant. Those societies moved in a lineal direction. Our society moves not only at a vastly accelerated rate but also outward in many directions, its movement centrifugal, not lineal. We have failed to recognize this change, this lack of unity. We continue to search for unity where no unity exists. We continue to think of the many directions as noise, or surface clutter. We think of the many directions as "transitory" rather than "constituent," and ignore the fundamental change. Surely the fact that we must look so hard and argue so long in our search for the dominant should reveal that change. The builders of Chartres or the Parthenon did not have to question or debate.

Thirdly, we must understand that not only do different directions exist but that the choice among them is individual and self-conscious. When we choose a manner of living or building we are aware of the many alternatives and aware, also, that we are making a choice. In the past, not only were alternatives restricted by limited techniques and materials, by ignorance and cultural inhibitions, but choices were hardly recognized as being choices. Other ages felt rather than knew.

These are the factors that have shaped our architecture. What we call chaos is simply an inevitable and natural result of these forces. Architecture will not achieve permanence in a time of accelerating change. It will not achieve unity in a time of diversity, nor anonymity in a time of self-consciousness. Any honest spontaneous expression of our time cannot now produce a style in the sense of the great historic styles. The absence of such a style is implicit in every aspect of our life. There remains, however, the question of what the architect's response should be. Is it more valuable to accept diversity, or to work for a style as a necessary means of providing some organization for the architecture of our time?

To answer this question we must understand the implications of a search for style, and understand the advantages and disadvantages the search might bring us.

A style imposes restraint upon the artist or architect. There are two levels of restraint that affect the artist. The first level is the one the conscientious artist imposes upon himself when undertaking any work. Internal within the single work of art, it is the restraint that makes a work self-consistent and unified: the restraint Picasso means when he calls art the sum of destruction, that Mies means when he tells us that he throws out things dear to his heart because they do not fit. The second level is external to the individual work of art, the restraint that says, "There are many ways to build a building (or paint a painting)—I choose this way." The builders of the Greek temples chose external space and the post and beam; the Gothic cathedral builders chose internal space and the pointed arch. This second level of restraint is precisely what makes a style.

Such restraint in our time would be different from that which produced the great architecture of the past, when the restraints were primarily unconscious—the result not only of limited knowledge, materials, and technology but of an unexamined consensus about the goals and direction of society. Today no such consensus exists. Necessarily, then, the only restraint attainable would not be one based upon an unconscious expression of great and universal goals but a mutual self-restraint based upon a conscious decision about those goals. Furthermore, since society shows no signs of arriving at such a choice, it would, presumably, be left to architects to do so. As Constantinos Doxiadis has said, such a style would be established from the top of the building pyramid, through the gradual seeping down of unique individual solutions, and not through the slow upward refinement of a vernacular building style as in the past. Understanding, then, the radically different framework through which a style would have to be established, it remains to ask whether such a style would be desirable.

The advantages of working in one definite style are obvious. When and while the style is vital it raises the level of individual accomplishment by enabling the artist to build upon the work of others. By offering the less than brilliant architect a consistent vocabulary in which to work, it enables him to design more competently. Lastly, of course, it enables architecture to become more than the sum of individual buildings, for surely, despite the brave claims of the architectural press, it is easier to build a beautiful and orderly city from one style than from many. (Whether a city is meant to be "beautiful" is another question.)

The disadvantages of searching for a universal style are less obvious. The acceptance of a common style certainly has never led to a loss of creativity for the architect, as the great ages of achievement prove. Nor does it mean monotony, so long as talented architects work within it. Restraint, of course, is a quality that each architect now expects only of other architects. But let us assume that a consensus based on restraint would be honored. There remains the more serious question of whether the style would be accepted by society. Maybe not. It might produce only an ineffective and incestuous architectural self-admiration society, resulting in loss of power, prestige, and, worst of all, commissions. But if the style were to be based not on whimsical "self-expression" but upon an honest desire to answer social needs, such losses could be borne with integrity. It is, after all, no sin for an architect to be at odds with society—he may in the long run be right. He may, too, be wrong—dead wrong. Just as the Victorian architects failed completely to identify the important forces of their culture, so might we. Being "wrong" is surely worse than being unpopular, but there are worse sins.

These arguments have traditionally been used to protest the idea of style. They have been used successfully and honestly to overturn the tyranny of styles that have become dead and meaningless. But none of them are, I think, valid in and of themselves. There is, however, another, more cogent argument against style, an argument based not on abstract principles of art history but upon the peculiar character of our own time. We know that the paths open to architecture are proliferating. They will not only continue to proliferate but will do so at an accelerating rate.

This proliferation is perhaps the constituent fact of our times. Now style, as we have seen, means restriction of direction. Today, it means saying, "Of the many paths opening to us, we shall choose only these; the rest we shall ignore." It means that as the paths proliferate, and grow, and fork, architecture will be exploring proportionately fewer and fewer of them. This is a very different thing from the choices made by architecture in the past. For it is not a matter of architecture and society choosing one path from a few open to them; it is a matter of society choosing to explore many paths, while architecture devotes itself to one, or to a very, very few. But the proliferation of choice is significant beyond its own self. It signals, I think, a new world to come, a revolution—the third great revolution, as drastic and as universal as the urban revolution of the third millennium BC and the Industrial Revolution of the eighteenth and nineteenth centuries. What kind of world it will bring, what the world of 2066 will be like, we cannot know. We can know only that it will be as different from ours as the nineteenth-century world of Pittsburgh or Birmingham was different from ancient Athens, as different as that Athens was from a pre-urban Mesopotamian village. With new means of communication, it may be a world without cities. With incredibly advanced energy sources, materials, transport technology, and climate control, it may be a world without the rigid, inert, ground-rooted shells we know as architecture. The paths leading most directly to that world are not visible now; perhaps they do not even exist as yet.

Now in such a time, to search for style, to explore one path and ignore the many, will inevitably isolate architecture from society, will make of it an ingrown and ineffective force. To follow one of the paths we see clearly now (and a style can only be based on such a path) will almost certainly ensure our missing those paths which might, through luck and insight, lead to the future.

It is no sin to be unaccepted, and not that much of a sin to be wrong. But is perhaps a sin to make sure that we will be wrong. A style, after all, is supposed to express the Zeitgeist of a time. And perhaps the Zeitgeist of our time is not so much a single idea as the proliferation of ideas. Perhaps our time is not so much a time as the forerunner of a time. Perhaps, indeed, the only style that can truly and honestly express our time is no style, but rather the abandonment of style for exploration.

There are two alternatives open to us. One is to search ardently for a style. The search, if successful, will produce more orderly and unified cities; will produce a higher level of individual accomplishment, will produce, in a word, more "beauty." But it will also mean a drawing back from the exciting prospects before us. The second alternative is to explore as many paths as possible, to explore aesthetically each new material and each new structural and lighting and environmental control system; to explore, as in the baroque, the myriad of complex spatial arrangements our technology makes possible. But accepting the second alternative also means accepting, however reluctantly, "chaos." It means insisting upon that first level of restraint which demands internal consistency within the work of architecture, but abandoning that higher-level restraint which achieves a consistent relationship between individual works. It means accepting the fact that our cities, however beautiful their individual parts, will never be a sum of beauty greater than those parts. But it may mean that we have pointed the way to a new world. We cannot anticipate the architecture of the future, but at least we can try not to hinder its development.

◢ ◢ ◢ ◢ Green Chaos

Over the millennia we have drifted from Earth Goddess to Dame Nature to environmental ethics to Gaia to . . . now what? *Wonders of the Serengeti* on educational television for the earnest lay audience and debate over the "role of nature in postmodern society" for design academics? Maybe less introspection? Maybe more plants?

I first went to the Climatron at the Missouri Botanical Garden in the mid-1960s, but it has taken me fifty years and this reminiscence to distill its essence: less a design than an experience. The experience is immersion, sensory abandonment, submission to an almost primeval overload of plants, smells, and humidity. It is a northern European fantasy of nature as a sensual engulfment . . . one can almost see the Green Man. And high above this dense botanical mass, what John Fowles called "green chaos," is the superrational, ultrareductionist, high-tech, spiderweb glass roof. We are in a half-cerebral, half-affective interplay of the natural and the artificial, an inversion of real and unreal, with the human-made appearing beyond the vegetal.

The Climatron seems a closing statement to the centuries-long design exploration of enclosing greenery for sensual delight and intellectual pride. The great Victorian conservatories played to that theme, but typically the Victorians celebrated with excess, extravagant expressions of nature—romancing, classification, iron and glass and heating technology, imperialist exploration and collection, and above all confidence. At the Crystal Palace and Chatsworth, nature and architecture were in balance, both clamoring for attention and admiration. In this sense the Climatron is an ending . . . the architectural technology is so potent that its formal spatial expression is gossamer-like, modest, and minimal. Technology has let nature win.

❧ ❧ ❧ ❧ What History Should We Teach and Why?

Landscape architecture faculties seem increasingly concerned with the role of history, in design and in the curriculum. Part of this interest is probably a cycle of fashion: a reaction against the modern movement's abandonment or debasement of history. Part is increasing intellectual sophistication among our landscape architecture departments, a dissatisfaction with history based on sabbatical slides. Part might be spillover from the revival of historical forms in postmodern architecture. No small part of it is the pressure upon landscape architectural faculty to produce something "scholarly," which often means amateurish history cum cultural geography.

This renewed interest raises a number of questions, some of which have been around for a long time. Is one undergraduate history course enough? If not, what should the following courses be and what is their relationship to one another? Should "the" history course continue to follow the five-hundred-years-of-Western-civilization-a-month model? And what is a history course? The three courses I teach all deal with the landscape in different periods, and major parts are organized chronologically, but this does not make them history courses. Should history be devoted to learning the details and craft of a profession or should it be a general education elective for all units? (Too often the answer is both, in the same course, naturally.) Is the standard introduction to landscape architecture course basically a history course with a few token visiting practitioners? Should it be? If the history course is to seriously inform our students' design, is it best given at the beginning of their studio track or is it more provocative and useful at the end? These are simple and obvious questions, familiar to all of us. There are, however, some more basic issues of the what and why of history.

Our Distinctive Use of History

History is a microcosm of our profession and our discipline. For the last quarter of a century, many things have been added to it and almost nothing deleted. As an example, consider what the terms Paleolithic period, pastoralism, patio homes, peasants, pesticides, plank roads, postmodernism, pre-Colombian landscape, and protoliterate culture have in common. They all start with the letter *p* and seem vaguely related to landscape history. Beyond that? They are all terms found in the subject index of Philip Pregill and Nancy Volkman's text but not in Norman Newton's. Our additions to history reflect both a broader view of the landscape as a complex social phenomenon and current political correctness. Most striking to me is the invasion of the "ordinary landscape," those landscapes not professionally designed, into courses that were once solely devoted to high, or elite, design. As with our profession and our discipline, we need to begin to consider letting go, or at least focusing or prioritizing.

Our history courses have been almost invariably taught by an amateur, usually a designer who also teaches studio. There are, after all, few academic historians specializing in landscape architectural matters, and even fewer savvy enough about the design process to earn their keep in the typical landscape architectural curriculum. This will probably change somewhat as the pressure for faculty with PhDs continues to escalate, but the amateur-historian instructor will be part of our scene for a long while yet. This is not necessarily bad. History should inform design and vice versa. "Amateur," after all, comes from the Latin root for love. Sensitivity, enthusiasm, and a deep conviction of the link between history and design are no small gifts. But consider that this situation would be unthinkable in the typical fine arts curriculum, the kingdom of art history specialists, and is in fact becoming increasing rare at architectural schools, too. Often the more fashionable the architectural school, the more specialized PhD historians on its faculty. Whatever the benefits and negatives of amateurism, they should lead to some self-examination vis-à-vis our peers.

Comparison with the role of history in still other disciplines and professions is instructive. As with architecture, highly specialized doctoral-level expertise and defensible turf are extreme in many disciplines, particularly in the humanities. The common organization of literature in the university consists of watertight isolation by genre and period (and often by "culture" today), a triumph of format and chronology over meaning. In contrast, history plays no significant role in the education of engineers and bench scientists. When the history of engineering or the history of physics is taught, it's usually in a seminar for honor students. Recently, some socially conscious medical schools have introduced courses in the sociology of medicine, courses that often have historical aspects. In law, history is a rare, arcane specialty, set aside at the LLD level for maybe one lawyer in hundreds. But if course catalog listings would indicate that the study of legal history is nonexistent, in some ways our own system of common law *is* the study of history, in which precedents *make* law. In the social and behavioral sciences, such as anthropology, sociology, and geography, history is commonly taught as an intellectual entry into concepts of the discipline for graduate students.

How then did history become an indispensable requirement for education in our discipline and simultaneously a subject that almost anyone can teach when faculty rotations are required? The simplest answer is continuity from Beaux-Arts education. Landscape architectural education, at least in the design-linked genealogy, began in those Beaux-Arts academies. Architecture has done more than we have to question or change the place of history in the schools, probably partly because of their larger mass and the development of architectural history as a specialty. History, not just historicism, was considered an oppressor by the radicals of the Bauhaus, when modernism became convention in architecture schools. The forms of the European masters were quickly adopted by the more progressive architectural schools but not their political or antihistorical philosophy or polemics. We teach history because we somehow know it's valuable, and because we took it when we were in school. There are probably worse reasons, but the questions remain. What history should we be teaching and why?

Commandments for Any History We Teach

Let me offer a few personal commandments relevant for any history we teach. I am discussing the undergraduate history that is instrumental, a functional part of education to be a professional or pedagogical landscape architect. I am not dealing here with courses preparing one to be a scholar of landscape history, or liberal arts courses, important as they are.

Our history must make a difference. The history we teach must be relevant to design. It must make the student reflect upon decisions that she makes in the design process. The correspondence of John Evelyn per se is a subject for scholars but not the studio designer, but the availability and use of plants that the letters reveal is of relevance to our design history.

It must not be *bad* history. This role I propose for history, isolating it from specialized work, can also isolate it from the knowledge of informed scholarship. While history does not have to deal with each current nuance of scholarly study, it must not be simply wrong or superficial, passing on lore of decades ago, currently rejected or questioned by scholars. Often it does. Other habits often lead us into teaching bad history. Eclecticism might be a strength, naïveté is not. In our enthusiasm to cover the breadth of landscape study, we often turn to currently fashionable books of dubious authenticity. A book becomes hot from many sources, from *Newsweek* for the least sophisticated of us (remember Alvin Toffler?), for those precious few of us, the *New York Review of Books*. We have bought into some very bad and or irrelevant stuff. Before we accept currently popular books in anthropology, sociology, popular culture, or whatever, we should ask ourselves whether we would give Charles Moore, Gerald Allen, and Donlyn Lyndon's *The Poetics of Gardens* to architectural students, as an example of the best in contemporary landscape design thinking.

Serious questioning of our history is different from trendy revisionism. Landscape architects are too genuine and too naive to pass on some of the absurdities of revisionism found in the current art world, but our good intentions often do produce an overlay of fashionable phrases, concerns, and disclaimers. Our canon is biased and arbitrary. Whose is not? Our job is to encourage our students to ask questions of it, and to develop their ability to do so. It is not to ask those questions to ourselves and then supply the students with currently fashionable answers. We should turn to other traditions, not for models, not for vocabularies, but as stimulus for reflection on our own habits. Literary criticism, for example, is of less value to us for its content than for its sense of important intellectual cycles, cycles that we are unaware of in our own work. Terry Eagleton offered this kind of valuable insight in noting that the last 150 years of literary criticism could be divided into roughly three equal periods. The first was biographical and concentrated on the author, the second structural and concentrated on the text, and the third contextual and concentrated on the reader. Are we still mired in that first phase?

Beware of the reification of culture. Contemporary anthropologists point out that culture is less a "real" phenomenon than a mental construct that we have erected to help us analyze the world. "Culture" is neither a monolith nor a black box. Society arrives at a culture and ideology as a product of interaction and transaction among agents, interests, and institutions. Generalizations about culture and its relationship to landscape are not necessarily bad if they are phrased with caution, and as interpretations. Too often when we refer to culture we are referring only to the collective taste and ideology of the power structure and patronage that sponsors art and shapes the most visible landscapes.

Whenever possible, study landscapes that can be experienced. The essence of landscape is change, a fact we find hard to admit. Studying real landscapes brings us face to face with their flux and their messages. It keeps us honest. Looking at landscapes that are out there, evolving and changing, also allows us to draw insights, particularly from our students. The landscape they see is often one to which we are blind, but it is just as real. Working in a real landscape gives their insights a better chance to vie with ours.

Be much clearer about the relationship we posit between the high and the ordinary landscapes, between the designed and the common. I am struck by the introduction of the vernacular (common, ordinary, pop, whatever) landscape into our history course. As someone who has made his intellectual living off this subject, I can hardly object to students studying it. But I am not clear myself what lessons for designers are to be learned from that changing "high"/"ordinary" relationship. I can think of many reasons for looking at the ordinary landscape in and for itself, but why within the standard history of landscape architecture course? The long-standing dichotomy between designed and nondesigned, or between high and ordinary (two very different distinctions, please note), is not only ill defined, but simplistic, misleading, and often false. The concepts behind these fuzzy distinctions could potentially lead to powerful insights about the social context of land and building. But it is not simple. Neither is it a subject for this essay but for a future one. What I ask for now is that teachers be clear and explicit, with themselves and with their students, about why certain landscapes are productive for study, be they professionally designed or not.

Fundamental Principles for Our History

Meaning is as important as form but is not inherent in form. Meaning does not come from a form. A form acquires meaning because of its place and function in a set of social or institutional values and systems (and sometimes, of course, personal history). These can be as broad as the Catholic Church of the Counter-Reformation or as narrow as a small clique of think-alike designers. Meaning is shaped and realized in a form; it withers, it is destroyed, it is often revised or reconstructed. Sometimes landscapes outlast the institutions and values that gave them meaning. Landscape, unlike literature, is not optional. Landscapes are not buildings either: they are more flexible, their interpretations wider, their access broader. Different groups, even different individuals, can read very different meanings into the same landscape. What meaning is recognizable or common to any significant group can be used and manipulated. The larger landscape and the larger society are not just context for our monuments; rather our designs are their creatures, even though either can outlive the other.

History is best thought of as irregular change, as a constant flow, varying in velocity and width, replete with streams, locks, dams, waterfalls, and swamps. Change is the essence, but change is not even . . . "change is lumpy" (I owe that bon mot to the late Peirce Lewis). The process of teaching history, or writing about it, or using it in the studio is the process of freezing, slicing, and abstracting bits, chunks that we define. How was the Renaissance landscape experienced by those who lived in it? Was our concept of renaissance even meaningful to them? In 2050 will the Donell Garden and Harlequin Plaza be considered part of the same historic style? Freezing time, stop framing, is a powerful tool of analysis. It is also much like the process of design itself; a building or a garden is itself a freezing of time. But the stuff in between can be just as important. We constantly note, and deplore, the pace of change, but somehow fail to accept it as a landscape given. Change, indeed, is at the core of landscape, whether almost glacially slow, or so rapid as to defy understanding or control, as it is now in much of the urbanizing third world. Abstraction from time might be necessary for teaching and learning, but it needs not to be confused with reality. We might all ask ourselves whether the history we teach is more like an album of still photos, a carefully edited film, or a kind of video verité.

While history might be made from massive, irresistible forces of near universality (it might not be either), those forces are given concrete shape by local contingencies. Nowhere is this truer, or as central, as in landscape. Landscape, as J. B. Jackson has noted, is human history on the land. It is local expression of larger than local forces. Those forces, today, are often far beyond the control of the shapers of any particular landscape, but their impacts on a particular place are distinctive. The common, the ordinary, and the monotonous reflect the broadest of cultural forces. But variety is also key, not for the sake of variety in itself, but because historical change takes place in a specific landscape. We need to study the local and the distinctive as well as the universal and the dominating.

All these general remarks pertain to any history we might teach. They still do not answer the what and when. What history do we teach? How do we arrive at that decision? I have no prescriptions, but I can offer an approach and some suggestive examples.

Three Alternative Directions

The history we teach must depend upon who we want to be. If our history courses are instrumental to our roles as professionals, then they should sharpen our performance in those roles. This is equally true of learning from history. The questions we pose, too often dominated by convenience, the conventions of academia, and current trends, should be relevant to what we need to know to do our job better. What is that job? We should abandon our self-generated image of "captain of the design team" and speculate upon how history could support more focused roles for a landscape architect. Three roles worth exploring come to mind: the landscape architect as a form giver, as a professional embedded in a society, and as an intervener, a manager of change upon the land. These roles lead to a history of form, to a social history, and to a history of landscape change.

Take the role of form giver first. The appropriate history might concentrate on works now in the canon, but it would approach them differently. It might begin as a conventional studio problem by setting up the program given to the original designer. That program is not always directly available, but piecing it together would itself be a learning experience. The next step in the process would be to link program to solution, to critique the match, and to develop alternative design solutions to the same problem and then to evaluate them. If, instead of an endless series of beautifully crafted chipboard models of Villa Lante, we developed alternative solutions through computer graphics, in effect staging a design competition with feedback, what might we learn? But many other questions could be asked about the development, the construction, and the life of any project. What historic formal prototype solutions were available to the designer? What was known and what not, what drawn upon and what rejected? Were the commission and the resultant landscape typical for the time? Did the landscape in turn become a prototype, or was it a breeding anomaly in the evolution of a form? What materials went into that landscape, what crafts and what types of labor built it? How did the joinery work? What was the riser-tread ratio? What could we learn about analyzing riser-tread ratios, à la Fletcher Steele, from the landmarks of landscape architectural history, from Villa Lante to the great pyramid at Tikal? What were the grades of the paths at Stourhead? How was a landscape cleaned, maintained, and refurbished? What were the original plants? In the case of the Alhambra, for example, no one knows, but what were the possibilities for those plants, and for their location and installation?

What plant palette was available to the designer? Were those plants "native," or the products of regional or transregional commerce, or brought by a conquering group? How might the planting have changed over time, and why? A comparative analysis of the four or five works that would be so studied would culminate that semester. This intensive study could create not only artists and craftsman but connoisseurs of the landscape art.

An alternative vision of the landscape architect is that of a professional whose work both serves and expresses the values of the society in which she works. While the product is still form, we would study the social context of the design in order to discuss "meaning." The emphasis would be not on what forms have been produced but on how those forms served a society and attained meaning within a given context. How can one understand why the Alhambra took on the shape and text it did without understanding the culture of Moorish Islam, and the system of authority in palace, household, and harem? If the first path is a history of form, this is a social history, or a history of meaning. It views the landscape not as a one-off tour de force but as an artifact created, maintained, and evolved in a cultural context. As the first history concentrated on a few built designs, so would this. But this course would also focus on a period or a genre. We would pick periods, or types, in which values and social organization, and hence meaning, were in flux. One example is the English garden from Stourhead to the formal-versus-natural debates at the beginning of the twentieth century. This history would take us from country estates to crystal palaces, from the refined taste of a handful of Augustan aesthetes to the rise of the industrial rich and the new bourgeoisie, to imperialism and colonialism, to exploration and plant discovery, collection, and classification, to plate glass and moist heat and cast iron, and through the changes of meaning connected with such social and technological transformations.

Or, we might study Central Park as a design, as a public pastoral interlude, and as a creature of politics, taste, and social values including those of class, moving from the original program controversies to such "current" issues as personal safety and fear of crime, both originally concerns of Olmsted himself.

This course must take examples from cultures and societies contrasting with our own, such as a Chinese Scholar's garden like the Wang Shi Yuan. Inquiry beyond our own tradition highlights the various ways in which form attains meaning under varying combinations of economics, ideology, technology, and social hierarchy. It would also expose the filters with which we have always viewed such work, filters peculiar to our own society, filters that change as our society changes. Few forms of landscape exhibit this more clearly than the Chinese Scholar's garden. Any intelligent, reasonably skeptical reading of the thousands of pages of materials that Westerners have produced could show how little we really know about how the users of these gardens perceived them, valued them, and felt about them. The selection of a few examples of the Scholar's garden, as shorthand for almost two thousand years of an art form in such a complex and highly developed society, is naive and misleading. The same forms and arrangements have been dismissed by Westerners as vulgar, silly, and lacking order in one period only to be romanticized and rhapsodized over as "a beyond rational unity between person and nature" in another. And is it really likely that Chinese gardens changed hardly at all over those centuries? Fiction and literature might be just as useful as scholarly analysis in the treatment of these works, showing us not only that the perceived meanings of gardens change across cultures and centuries but that any interpretation tells us as much about the culture making it as the culture "studied." This is necessary prelude for richer, deeper understanding.

The third vision of the landscape architect is expressed in the subtitle of *Landscape Journal,* "The Planning and Design and Management of the Land," all of which include intervention. The most significant mark of our contemporary landscape is rapid change. Establishing a fit between human and natural systems, then, means guiding and managing landscape change. So this landscape history would concentrate on place change. We would view history, not as a series of incidents, but as a process of change. Process would come first, products second. While much change is globally driven, the study of such forces is the province of social, economic, and political historians. But as mentioned earlier, no matter how strong the global forces of change, they take their particular forms within specific landscapes. As they modify those landscapes, so the landscape and the local culture modify the products of that change, and make them specific to a place. If we believed this, then we could most productively concentrate on the history of particular landscapes, from geological and vegetative origins, to aboriginal inhabitants, to the process of different groups in societies moving through and shaping cultures, on down to our postmodern, almost-placeless, being upon the land. Here again, cross-cultural comparisons would deepen our understanding.

Vineyards are a good example. Wherever in the world we find the classic category of a Mediterranean climate, characterized by warm moist winds in winter and dry summers, grapes have been grown and wine made. The landscape of vine and wine is as intimate, compelling, and demanding a bond as exists between human and nature, and as place-specific. Not only can wine grapes be grown only in certain climates, but every microaspect of the site affects their quantity and quality: long- and short-term temperature and rainfall, steepness of slope and its attitude toward sun, the local soil, the microdrainage, the presence or absence of moisture at night, and so on. This microecology is summed in the word *terroir.* Grower and vintner learn to work with what they cannot change, and manipulate what they can. Terracing, trellising, planting, spacing, and pruning all become more than science, more than craft, transcend into an art. And as all landscape-people relationships are to some degree indeterminate, the grapes and the growers are subject to the vagaries of nature.

What better case study could there be than such landscapes? Think of the Napa Valley, product of our own West and its myth of California as lotus land. Mountain boundaries open to the bay at the south; sequential occupation by American Indians, ranchers, the rich retreating from San Francisco, wine growers, winemakers; and, since the early '90s, sadly and apparently triumphantly, urbanization. It's all there, from splendor of the terrain to the enormous variability of *terroir*, from functional vernacular to postmodern monuments, from conflicts between grape growers and winemakers to the politics of development and environmental response that make strange bedfellows and new landscapes. We could compare Napa with other winemaking regions of the world, say the Medoc and Burgundy. Three different regions, committed to intensive winemaking for 50, 250, 750 years, respectively, but developed under different political, economic, and transportation regimes. California emphasizes process, technology, and science, the others the fruit and "the spirit of the place" (i.e., terroir). Today all three resonate one to the other in technology, trade, and craft, all in a global culture overlying unique places.

The way to learn about the human landscape is to study it in terms of people in a place and not monuments, styles, and period or even "honest vernacular." A final advantage of studying the history of change in a specific place is that the relationship between the "high" and the "ordinary" can be more productively explored, for the relation between them, however defined, is first of all a matter of social and physical context. If landscape is the imprint of human history, it is too important to be left to antiquarians and genealogists of the county historical society. (It is probably obvious that this third course is the one that I would choose to teach.)

Conclusion

Each of you might try inventing your own such course. I know that some of you already have. The courses I suggested overlap and share common material. Maybe the distinction between them is not always clear. But the essential difference is that of a single conceptual focus on how to understand a landscape, even what a landscape is. It is that focus which gives a framework (not a theory) that fits facts together into an integrated understanding. The point is not to advocate these three particular courses but that our history courses should depend on what we want to do. If we can't decide what we want to do, or think we can do almost everything, our history courses will reflect this, to our detriment. And just as our own history courses should reflect our view of the profession, so should we evaluate the relation between landscape history as an instrumental course aimed at future professionals, and landscape history as a liberal arts course aimed at a broad range of students. To assume that the same course can serve both audiences, as we commonly do, is a recipe for failure.

Our history courses must have rigor. They must not be "bad" history, but scholarship that can be tested and built upon. They must have a focus appropriate to what we see as our role. Such focus requires conviction, but need not entail bigotry, intolerance, or revealed dogma. (My own history course under Alfred Caldwell suffered from all three, but proved to me that fanatical beliefs beat no beliefs at all.) Students should be encouraged to question the tenets and assumptions of the course and to discuss them. Exposure to strong views, accompanied by a demand to think and to respond, is more likely to produce mission and direction than are permissive and passive recitals of designers, dates, gardens . . . and a bit of environmental consciousness.

Developing such courses is a daunting task. Some of the material (not much) is in our hands. Other parts can be gleaned (very respectfully, please) from other disciplines. Other parts we ourselves will have to investigate. We will have to integrate and focus. But in a time when the tenure process deems publishing more important than teaching, designing, or building, in a time when such publishing is often bibliographical minutiae or descriptive geography rephrased, isn't this a challenge for real scholarship for a relevant mission?

❦ ❦ ❦ ❦ Sex in the Garden

One concise definition of the garden is a place where nature is controlled to serve at, and for, human pleasure. If the jungle is a symbol of sex beyond human control and the lawn a symbol of sex corseted and overcontrolled, then the garden is a place where sex is available for human delight in a controllable context. Sexuality exists there within a frame of human civility, much like the sensual drift of Gertrude Jekyll's plants within the framework of Edwin Luyten's masonry. The darker side of sex is only occasionally hinted at, as in the drawings of Aubrey Beardsley, the novels of John Fowles, or in Rumer Godden. The celebration of the garden as both a metaphor and a literal place for sex has been a theme of literature from the Song of Solomon through the Arabian Nights to a contemporary poem of Anthony Hecht, who says of the Villa d'Este, "Here is cause for the undiminished bounce of sex . . . there is no garden to the practiced gaze half so erotic." Where did all that go, I wonder? Where now are Marlowe's man-like satyrs, who once in the garden "with their goat feet danced the antic hay"? Drinking a mojito in a Home Depot hot tub?

❦ ❦ ❦ ❦ Dreams of Tomorrow

There was a time not long ago, say from 1910 through 1930, when architects dreamed of what would be possible when the hoped-for promises of new knowledge and new technologies were fulfilled. That time is gone. Very few any longer dream of what architecture might be; by our rational standards an architecture without restrictions of client, budget, program, or existing technology is hardly architecture at all.

As the horizons promised by science and technology have expanded, the dreams, curiously, have shrunk; architects have turned to romantic facadism and timeworn concepts of "civic design." But in science fiction the dreams have lived on and grown. Today's science fiction is very unlike its early bug-eyed-monster-and-nubile-maiden phase. The best of science fiction is now as well written as any popular writing. As its style has changed, so has its orientation. Science fiction today pays less and less attention to space opera adventures and more and more turns to sociological and political speculation.

The result has been a progressive blurring of the already hazy border separating science fiction from mainstream literature. If any one quality distinguishes science fiction today, it is the fact that its ideas are not only more imaginative but more serious than those one can generally find elsewhere in popular fiction. But despite the burdens of seriousness and respectability, science fiction writers still dream; it is their job. In their dreams of far times and far places, under skies of unfamiliar clouds and colors, beneath strange mountains and beside strange seas, they see buildings and cities. And those buildings and cities are more wonderful than any that architects dream of.

The history of fantastic literature is filled with architectural imagery. Certain themes appear again and again: dreams of pastoral simplicity; of unrelieved geometric purity; of geomorphic spaces; of fairy-tale grottoes and flowery castles indistinguishable from the mountains from which they rise; of Arabian Nights pleasure cities of jeweled columns, domes, playing water, and scented gardens; of vast spaces where stairs and ramps intertwine in Piranesian complexity. To this traditional store of images, science fiction has added ideas based upon scientific and technological predictions, ideas that go far beyond architects' ideas of what might be achieved.

Science fiction writers have dreamed of sensual effects possible with a far advanced understanding of the basic physics of materials: walls instantly changeable from opaque to translucent or transparent, closing off a room, flooding it with filtered light, or throwing it open to the outside, all at the flick of a switch; luminescent surfaces glowing with a soft diffused light, containing moving patterns of changing colors at different depths; walls that change their surface shapes like waterfalls; floors that change their textures from glassy smoothness to furry richness with the movement of people. F. Scott Fitzgerald's "The Diamond as Big as the Ritz" contains several such splendid displays. He and many other writers have created the descendants of the Arabian Nights pleasure palaces.

Light effects figure frequently in science fiction. One writer describes a rotating lens that focuses a constant beam of sunlight on an altar standing alone in a dark temple. Another pictures a future art form in which patterns of light are composed on a screen like moving paint—formed, changed, and erased from an electronic console. Still another dreams of creating light from the air itself, lighting gardens and whole parks with a rose-tinged silvery glow.

Dreams of structural and engineering perfection are even more common. Self-contained light, power, and sanitation units make houses independent of fixed exterior utilities. Lighter than air, or equipped with antigravity devices, they move anywhere, anytime. New building materials are envisioned, ranging from just a little beyond our present capabilities to the truly fantastic. One example: a small package—open it, add water, and materials flow from it and expand in minutes to form the floor, walls, roofs, and windows of a complete house. Climate control is, of course, a science fiction necessity for life on other worlds. Indeed, these dreams may not be so fantastic; in our own world the advanced climate controls of a few years hence may be a feedback from systems developed for use in space.

Science fiction worried about automation long before it became a matter of practical concern. Ray Bradbury has written several haunting descriptions of its effects on architecture:

They walked down the hall of their soundproofed, Happylife Home, which had cost them thirty thousand dollars installed, this house which clothed and fed and rocked them to sleep and played and sang and was good to them.

The sun was setting. The house was closing itself in, like a giant flower, with the passing of the light . . .
. . . In the dawn the sun, through the crystal pillars, melted the fog that supported Ylla as she slept. All night she had hung above the floor, buoyed by the soft carpeting of mist that poured from the walls when she lay down to rest. All night long she had slept on this silent river, like a boat upon a soundless tide. Now the fog burned away. The mist level lowered until she was deposited on the shore of wakening.

One of the strangest of science fiction buildings is the "Psychotropic House"—set, reasonably enough, in Los Angeles. This house joins automation and advanced materials technology to a far advanced science of psychology. The result is a house that senses its owner's moods and automatically adjusts to them: changing its colors, scenting its air, playing music, expanding and becoming transparent or shrinking and closing itself in as those moods vary.

One even more fantastic creation is based on a breakdown of the borderline between organic and inorganic processes: Bradbury's Martian village that not only grows houses out of living matter but secretes food, water, and showerbaths for its inhabitants—the end result of truly organic architecture. Another idea postulates a similar breakthrough between the conventional concepts of force and matter, and constructs a city from fields of pure energy, now solid, now transparent, always changing color and shape.

A science capable of such accomplishments would surely reshape physical patterns of living as well. With their new buildings, science fiction writers dream of new cities and new landscapes; their dreams echo both the hopes and the doubts of professional planners.

The most commonly imagined city is remarkably like the Ville Radieuse of Le Corbusier. Great slender white towers, chaste and aloof, rise from manicured parks, and are linked one to another with graceful ribbon-like motorways. Often the motorways disappear, and transport becomes a matter of individual air scooters or antigravity belts.

The other common science fiction picture of the city is the supercity—today's Manhattan extrapolated to an appalling density of people and buildings. H. G. Wells portrayed it first in 1907 in his novel of the future *When the Sleeper Wakes*. The image starts with tall skyscrapers linked together by roads and ramps at all levels. It ends as a city where lawns and parks, streets and houses disappear. The city becomes one monster superbuilding. Millions, perhaps a billion, people are born in it, live in it, and die in it, never leaving it for an hour. It is a structure of hundreds of stories above ground and as many below, a matrix of moving roadways, walkways, and conveyor belts. It becomes not a dream, but a nightmare.

Science fiction sees us settling the sea as we have the land. As the oceans are farmed and grazed to feed the earth's growing population, buildings invade the seas. Great bubbles holding millions of people float on the surface, anchored to the bottom or moving about under their own power. Domes and vaults cover the ocean floors. People live and die under the water, dwelling in self-powered, doughnut-shaped structures, moving with their work or joining together to form colonies.

Finally, as man moves far from earth, great migrant space bubbles evolve: cities containing thousands of people, moving through galaxies following the demands of interstellar trade and labor.

The best of science fiction deals not only with the architectural gadgetry of a glamorous superscience and supertechnology but with human and social side effects. One might expect science fiction to be filled with predictions of glorious human happiness achieved through man's increasing power to shape and change the world about him. Indeed, this is partly true; there is a sense of the wonder and magic promised by science. But another theme runs through much of contemporary science fiction, a theme of doubt and distrust, a troubled questioning of our ability to control the science we create. Like the puritan whose conscience hurts when everything else feels good, the science fiction writer cannot convince himself that the marvels created will make anyone happy. He is afraid that man, like Frankenstein, will be destroyed by his own ingenuity.

The buildings and cities that he creates turn from dreams into nightmares. A real lion emerges from the 3-D nursery veldt scene to eat the parents who are trying to turn the power off. The organic Martian village, built to feed and clothe its original inhabitants, now vanished, is unable to adapt to human biology. It transforms the hapless space traveler into a snouted, four-footed Martian. The automated house burns itself out attempting to please its former owners, whose radiation-etched shadows are seared into its walls. And the marvelous machine city, built to serve man, turns him into a spineless automaton; surviving him, it goes on repeating its now senseless tasks for eternity.

This ambivalent attitude, a glorification of science and technology hedged by doubts of our moral ability to control our creations, shows up clearly in the science fiction writer's view of the city. The two archetypal dreams, the Ville Radieuse and the supercity, are perceived very differently. The Ville Radieuse in science fiction is a glamorous symbol of humanity's ability to assimilate technical skills in a healthy way. It is a happy, prosperous place where our power over our environment produces a comfortable, idyllic life. The supercity, in contrast, is a place of terror, people degraded, pleasure-seeking ciphers, a minor entry in the computers that order the city's life. The below-ground levels of the superbuilding become a proletarian cesspool for the use of those lucky or cunning enough to live on the highest levels. Wells saw it so in 1907; Isaac Asimov in a 1956 novel called the supercities *Caves of Steel*. In Asimov's city, the citizens—quartered in cramped cubicles, fed in vast automated community kitchens—are so degraded and urbanized (words often synonymous in science fiction) that the sight of open sky or naked sun produces panic.

Nowhere in science fiction does the Ville Radieuse plan of high-rise towers and large landscaped parks produce the kind of gang rule Jane Jacobs attributes to it. Seldom, on the other hand, does the supercity produce the civilized, sophisticated life we associate with the great urban centers of the Western world. Where such traditionally urban pleasures are described, they are confined to the lucky elite, or isolated in some exotic port on a distant world, some faintly sordid pleasure place for space-roving roisterers and playboys. The logical conclusion of this idea of the evil city is a race so advanced in technology, psychokinesis, and behavioral science—and so powerfully in control of their environment—that they abandon their cities and choose to live in small villages of bare huts, practicing primitive-seeming rites for emotional fulfillment. Perhaps science fiction writers, most of whom are British or American, suffer from historic national prejudices against the city. Certainly their views are curious echoes of current professional controversy.

Realization of many of these dreams lies centuries in the future. Others surely will never come true. But some might be realized in a few generations, or even a few years. The history of aeronautics and astronautics proves that predictions of the future consistently underrated the speed of scientific advance. Predictions fail, as Arthur C. Clarke has pointed out, from failure of nerve (the unwillingness to push available facts to their logical conclusion), and failure of imagination. In *Profiles of the Future* he writes, "Anything that is theoretically possible will be achieved in practice no matter what the technical difficulties, if it is desired greatly enough."

The visions of future architecture in science fiction are not now "desired greatly enough." We prefer to spend our energy on arms, or on men on the moon. But with social and political change we may choose, in a not far away time, to spend comparable energy on housing, planning, and environmental control. If so, many of the science fiction dreams may, like more conventional predictions of the future, fail from being too conservative.

The architectural dreams of science fiction tell us three things: First, they warn us that technological advance may not produce better living conditions. Perhaps we cannot be reminded too often that even the most daring and high-minded proposals, when realized, are not necessarily guaranteed utopia.

Secondly, the dreams of science fiction, like those in all fantasy writing, remind us again that architecture has great potential for immediate sensual satisfaction, a fact that contemporary architecture has chosen to ignore until very recently. Literary romancing about architecture is a tricky thing; it is difficult to translate satisfactorily even into pictures, for the graphics in fantasy and science fiction are mostly flat and unsatisfying. Familiarity breeds lack of interest; attitudes change; yesterday's pleasure palace survives as an amusing relic. But the fault might lie not in the fact of dreaming, but in the nature of the dreams.

Science fiction offers us the dream that science and technology, properly controlled, can create not only a more comfortable and affluent world but a richer, more beautiful one. It is a dream troubled by doubts and misgivings, but one full of promise. Strangely, for a society otherwise obsessed with science, it is a dream that has interested only a few architects—Buckminster Fuller, Frei Otto, a handful of others.

This was not always so. In the 1920s the European avant-garde, Bruno Taut and others, based their visions firmly on the promise of technology. But as the promise has grown, the dreams have almost vanished. The trivial and unimaginative uses to which architecture has put technology might have tarnished the dream.

Success—the common acceptance of technology at all levels of society—could have itself destroyed the dream; but the acceptance of baroque spatial complexity and Victorian historical revivalism instead led to progressively wilder visions. Certainly today architects are dreaming, perhaps more than ever; project renderings in the architectural press are filled with a romance and fantasy unthinkable ten or twenty years ago. But the dreams have changed; they look backward, not forward. They are filled with open or half-concealed allusions to medieval town squares and Palladian villas. They are dreams that lead into blind alleys, into stylistic fads that last a year or two and pass.

The third message of science fiction, the one most important for architects, is the reminder that architectural dreaming can be a positive force.

Dreams, founded not on historical reveries but on the potentialities of science, are a response to those forces which are reshaping our world. Perhaps they might even help remedy those failures of imagination that inhibit predictions of the future, and so help us to see more accurately the shape of tomorrow's world.

Reprise

There was a time within memory, the 1950s and the 1960s, that has come to be called the "golden age of science fiction." In the later part of that time, however, science fiction began the largest change in its history. It moved into the mainstream. It would be nice to think that this was because we finally recognized the quality of the writing and the imagination of its scenarios. But in fact what changed the image of science fiction was neither writing nor authors but its transference, first to television and then to motion pictures. Think early *Star Trek* to recent *Avatar*. That high visibility has even been deemed worthy of attention in academia; popular culture faculty, reinforced with critical theory vocabulary, have busied themselves producing inane and arcane writings and courses best summed up as "Adorno takes on the Jedi." Other changes have been more positive. For the first time the best science fiction writers, formerly paid pennies per word by the cult rags and the few slicks, can now earn many times as much from the big book publishers, and the writing shows it.

The demise of the magazines took with it the traditional dramatic and often absurd illustrations in the pulps, the sketches in the better slicks, and those covers still treasured by collectors from the early days of the pulps. That public now aware of science fiction knows it on the screen, big or small. The new science fiction graphics, based on digital manipulation, are spectacular compared to their forerunners. Still, some old forms and norms persist. Buildings are still "built," and built with recognizable materials. The landscapes are more imaginative but usually composed of familiar elements combined in a new way, if on spectacular scale, particularly the urban visions. In an ironic failure of the imagination, these visions still have a feeling of the earliest science fiction illustrations, where buildings looked like the skyscrapers of the late nineteenth and early twentieth centuries but were serviced by vehicles operating at many levels, apparently unregulated by any traffic control, and likely to soon be emblazoned with Amazon or FedEx logos.

The magnificent urban scenes in *Attack of the Jedi* are a ready example of the limits and inconsistency of our imagination. The city's vision was one of glitter and levels and motions that make Las Vegas look like a Cotswold village. But the interiors look more like an art moderne first-class lounge in a 1930s transatlantic liner. Today, the most imaginative and striking science fiction illustrated dreams are of course based on 3-D visualization and many can be found on the Internet, once you wade through the mass of digitalized, sadomasochistic, alien sex sites. The most common vision of the future city resembles a vast mega oil refinery, not unlike a full-color, hyperscaled fruition of an Archigram dream of several decades ago. To see the best you must turn to some of the book compilations, particularly the digital masterpieces of Stephen Martiniere and Spart. But even here, there is a gestalt of traditional architectural images, revised but recognizable. Dematerialization of architecture is never even considered, and the luminescence of the plants in *Avatar* is one of the few examples of unpredictable landscape dreams. Where are the "non-buildings," the "impossible landscapes" . . . environments of shifting light, of opacity, transparency, and translucence, sounds merging with light and color to form patterns suggesting enclosure or openness?

That "golden age" of science fiction peopled deep space with shallow characters, but the opening line of one of those novels, Clifford Simak's *City*, ". . . these are the tales the dogs tell as they sit around the fire," sums up its sense of wonder. So do Ray Bradbury's tile-inlaid Martian canals, and Asimov's caves of steel, vast, oppressive, hermetically sealed structures, Soleri-like megastructures apparently designed by mechanical engineers and human resource officers. In the late 1960s and early 1970s science fiction turned to what is now called the "new wave." The "what if" of the future and its technology remained but was approached in the larger context of social setting and deeper character development. Characterized by social, economic, and political concerns and issues of class and status, sexuality and gender, the bright vision of brave new buildings and landscapes faded. It might be too strong to say that the dreams became nightmares and the utopias dystopias, but it is fair to say that this new writing excelled at turning opportunities into problems.

In the decades since there are two threads of science fiction imagination that should be fodder for designers. The first is "cyberpunk," which one critic has characterized as "high tech and low life." Often set in the very near future or even contemporary life, the major figures are hackers who cynically stand apart from the society around them and are often hooked up to computerized brains and limbs. The dividing line between person and avatar blurs. But cyberpunk does conjure up those new, almost dematerialized, visions of the environment missing for so long. Here are worlds shaped by sound and light and change, possible hints of what the highest tech areas of today's Berlin or Tokyo might become.

The other thread might be described as "eco sci-fi." Science fiction's concern with ecological systems began back in the 1970s with Frank Herbert's classic series, the *Dune* books, which focused on a distant desert-like world and the life forms it produced. But still, this was a given environment. It was left to Frank Robinson, in the *Mars Trilogy,* to speculate on evolving interactions between environmental change and social setting. The three books focus on the "terraforming" of Mars, not only the technological obstacles and successes but the attendant social and political travails, in a meticulously detailed and richly imagined chronicle that might well be required introductory reading for any environmentally oriented education or practice. Imagination is still "out there," it seems.

◢ ◢ ◢ ◢ Reflections on the Landscapes of Memory

Our interactions with the environment are shaped by our existence as an organism, as a member of a culture, and as individuals. The contention that our evolutionary history, our "memory" of the landscapes experienced as hominids, shapes our interactions with the environment is familiar in extrapolations of ethological work on spatial behavior. Occasionally questions of environmental preference or pleasure have also been explored in this evolutionary framework. Jay Appleton, in *The Experience of Landscape,* notes that our "preferred landscapes" offer both prospect and refuge (seeing without being seen), and he explains this as a memory of the optimal landscape for a mammal existing in a prey-predator chain.

Paul Shepard, in *The Tender Carnivore and the Sacred Game,* claims that our needs and pleasures in the landscape can be traced directly from a social and physiological heritage as hunters of large mammals:

> The past, having shaped our species, holds the clues to normal function. . . . Men need, in their non-human environment, open country with occasional cover, labyrinthine play areas, a rich variety of plants, animals, rocks, stars; structures and forms numbering into the thousands; initiation, solitude, transitional and holy places, a wide variety of food organisms and diversity of stone and wood, nearby fresh water, large mammalian herds, cave and other habitation sites, and so on.

The interaction between culture and environment is now being explored with a fervor that would have been unusual and unseemly a decade ago. Some current anthropological work can be thought of as a complex but convincing restatement of relationships discredited decades ago as environmental determinism. Others have described the cosmological structures of nonindustrialized societies in attempts to link them with our environmental attitudes and behaviors. A plethora of authors have discussed landscape attitudes and preferences linked to the cultural "memories" of England and the United States.

Personal Landscape History

The role of individual history has been studied less. Yet even those who emphasize phylogenetic and cultural imprints would admit that an individual's childhood leaves some environmental predispositions; a generation addicted to psychotherapy could hardly think otherwise. But if the subject has not been of common concern, a remarkable convergence of interest in it has recently taken place among those who study environmental values.

Sudden enthusiasm is no more valid a guide to merit than fashionable disdain. We need to examine this position and to ask what relevance the remembered landscape of our childhood has for understanding environmental satisfaction and for designing better environments.

To begin with, we must distinguish between environmental pleasure and environmental preference: the feel of wet grass underfoot or the joyful terror of empty echoing streets is environmental pleasure or pain, while the selection of a facade in mock Tudor instead of mock Georgian indicates a preference. I will avoid further definitions, and regretfully ignore several interesting questions, such as whether preference might be more culturally determined while pleasure more shaped by biological and personal history, and whether environmental preference is relatively constant, in contrast to pleasure, or slow to change or cycle, and is more likely to be satisfied through long-term adjustments such as locational decision.

Understanding the landscapes of memory—a term that I use to denote memories of places from personal, not cultural or evolutionary, childhood—might give us clues for producing more pleasurable places for children. Yet most of the innovative playground work of the last decade has emphasized more direct response to children as users, bypassing as far as possible the traditional layers of adult intervention.

Florence Ladd and Clare Cooper Marcus have noted that designers often perpetuate in their work settings in which they were particularly happy as children. If this tendency is common in designers and people involved in design decisions, it represents a constraint in achieving design responsive to its users.

Third, careful analysis of the landscapes of memory might identify universals of environmental experience, universals that stand out more clearly in memory, fantasy, or reverie than in the usual adult interaction with the landscape.

Last, the memorable landscapes of our childhoods might directly shape our adult responses by determining the nature of the pleasure or satisfaction that we will ever after obtain from the environment. Many design behavior scholars have advanced this position, but its most eloquent and perhaps extreme description comes from Wallace Stegner.

> Unless everything in a man's memory of childhood is misleading, there is a time somewhere between the ages of five and twelve which corresponds to the phase ethologists have isolated in the development of birds, when an impression lasting only a few seconds may be imprinted on a young bird for life. . . . Expose a child to a particular environment at this susceptible time and he will perceive in the shapes of that environment until he dies.

If this is true, then attention to the landscape of memory might yield knowledge that would help us design more pleasurable environments for all people.

This two-part assumption, that childhood environments shape later environmental pleasure and that proper understanding of this phenomenon could help guide environmental designers, is implicit in much of the current humanistic literature on the personal environment but seldom made explicit. These assumptions seem reasonable, but they are unproven and untested. They need scrutiny and testing, not unexamined acceptance. If memories of the childhood environment are worth attention, a ready supply is available in literature.

Landscapes of Literature

The landscapes of literature are diverse. There are evocations of the visual essence of the land, like Willa Cather's "Elsewhere the sky is the roof of the world; but here the earth is the floor of the sky." There are mood landscapes made from the long history of people and place, as in Lawrence Durrell's Alexandria, which is a place of heat, lethargy, and foreignness. There are mood landscapes made from the transitory interplay of setting with social symbolism or internal state of mind—the London, for example, of Anthony Powell, or T. S. Eliot, where "the winter evening settles down with smell of steaks in passageways." There are landscapes that never were, such as Coleridge's Xanadu and Baudelaire's imagined Paris as "that awe-inspiring landscape such as no mortal ever saw."

Archibald MacLeish's future landscape is another imaginary place:

. . . It is colder now,
               there are many stars,
                             we are drifting
North by the Great Bear,
               the leaves are falling,
The water is stone in the scooped rocks,
                          to southward
Red sun gray air:
          the crows are
Slow on their crooked wings,
                  the jays have left us:
Long since we passed the flares of Orion.

    ("Epistle to Be Left in the Earth")

Most important for our purposes are literary descriptions of place in which writers re-create the intensely personal landscapes of their own childhood by speaking directly or through fictional characters. James Agee provides such a passage in *A Death in the Family:*

> On the rough wet grass of the back yard, my father and mother have spread quilts. We all lie there, my mother, my father, my uncle, my aunt, and I too am lying there . . . on our sides, or on our backs. They are not talking much, and the talk is quiet, of nothing in particular, of nothing at all in particular, of nothing at all. The stars are wide and alive, they seem each like a smile of great sweetness, and they seem very near. . . . and who shall ever tell the sorrow of being on this earth, lying, on quilts, on the grass, in a summer evening, among the sounds of night.

Two warnings are in order. First, the examples I use are passages that have stayed in the mind from casual reading. They might not be representative; they might say more about my own inclinations or memories than about the personal landscapes of literature. Second, these authors might be telling us in a particularly evocative way what most people would tell us about their remembered landscapes if they were as articulate as novelists. But we cannot be sure that the landscapes of writers are representative of the common experience of humanity. The sensitivities that drive writers to their craft, or certain authors to describe their childhood landscapes, might not be representative, just as a remembered landscape that has been passed through the discipline and demands of expression on the printed page might be an unreliable guide to the real internal landscape of its author.

Such literary recollections of the child's landscape might offer clues to how or whether the landscape of memory shapes later satisfaction and whether implications for design exist. These remembrances commonly have two characteristics relevant to these questions.

First, in many descriptions what dominates memory is not place but mood, remembered emotion. The physical attributes of the environment might be described in detail, but they serve as a supportive setting for an introspective or social experience, not as primary sources of pleasure. Internal states of mind give power to these place memories, not direct visual or spatial experiences. The remembered emotions vary. Perhaps the most common is that which Agee described: secure comfort and protection experienced amid adult place and pastime. There are memories of what Agee called the "sick joy of fear," that sudden isolated pang of terror and exhilaration peculiar to late childhood and early adolescence. There are memories, too, of solitude and an introspective tranquility, as in Larry McMurtry's book *Horseman, Pass By:*

> When I knew Granddad was in bed I went back to the windmill and stopped the blades, so I could climb up and sit on the platform beneath the big fin. Around me, across the dark prairie, the lights were clear. The oil derricks were lit with strings of yellow bulbs, like Christmas trees. . . . I sat above it all, in the cool breezy air that swept under the windmill blades, hearing the rig motors purr and the heavy trucks growl up the hill. Above the chattering of the ignorant Rhode Island Reds I heard two whippoorwills, the ghostly birds I never saw, calling across the flats below the ridge.
>
> Sitting there with only the wind and the darkness around me, I thought of all the important things I had to think about: my honors, my worries, my ambitions. I thought of the wild nights ahead, when I would have my own car, and could tear across the country to dances and rodeos. I picked the boys I would run with, the girls we would romp; I kept happy thinking of all the reckless things that could happen in the next few years.

Sometimes place and feeling blend so strongly in these memories they become indistinguishable from each other. But although place is indelibly associated with the emotional experience in recall, it does not seem to have been its cause. A feeling of security is neither a baseball game nor a committee meeting, but an emotion that can arise in a child in any number of environments. Only with time and recall does the association between place and feeling become fixed and transformed into an internalized behavior setting of the emotions existing in the memory alone.

But if the environment did not produce the feeling in these memories, environmental stimuli once firmly associated with that emotion might be able to recall or re-create it. If so, that association would be vital for design, regardless of the original cause-effect relationship.

The second relevant aspect of these memories is the character of the environmental elements involved. Remembered landscapes are often built, not of bricks, buildings, and spaces of pleasing proportions, but of less material elements.

Sound is one. In the pages preceding Agee's descriptions of his back-yard, he lovingly built an evocation of a Memphis street at evening from the sounds of footsteps, trolley cars passing, and locusts echoing the soft, soothing sound of spraying hoses. An uncounted number of authors summon from remembrances of adolescence an empty late-night street where a terrible silence is broken by the quickly passing sound of the "lonely rhythmic clopping of a horse," or that peculiarly American symbol, the locomotive steam whistle.

The experience of changing seasons is often recalled, as is the changing of the day with its quality of light. In *A Walker in the City* Alfred Kazin writes:

> Now the light begins to die. Twilight is also the mind's grazing time. Twilight is the bottom of that arc down which we had fallen the whole long day, but where I now sit at our cousin's window in some strange silence of attention, watching the pigeons go round and round to the leafy smell of soupgreens from the stove. In the cool of that first evening hour, as I sit at the table waiting for supper and my father and the New York *World,* everything is so rich to overflowing, I hardly know where to begin.

In *Wolf Willow* Wallace Stegner evokes smell:

> It is with me all at once, what I am hoping to re-establish, an ancient, unbearable recognition, and it comes partly from the children and the footbridge and the river's quiet curve, but much more from the smell. For here, pungent and pervasive, is the smell that has always meant my childhood. I have never smelled it anywhere else, and it is as evocative as Proust's madeleine and tea.

Some of childhood's settings, recalled with affection and wonder, are landscapes unappealing or even repugnant to usual adult sensitivities. McMurtry's high plains landscape probably inspires little love in people driving through west Texas or viewing those films that capture it so well. Our own memories, and contemporary playground designers too, tell us of children's joy in unkempt lots. Kazin remembers freight yards and monument works and "the smell and touch of those 'fields,' with their wild compost under the billboards of weeds, goldenrod, bricks, goat droppings, rusty cans, empty beer bottles, fresh new lumber, and damp cement, lives in my mind as Brownsville's great open door, the wastes that took us through to the west."

Stegner remembers the town dump; Jean Shepherd remembers, with an affection that seems only partly ironic, the mill town fishing lake:

> The water is absolutely flat. There has not been a breath of air since April. It is now August. The surface is one flat sheet of old used oil laying in the darkness, with the sounds of the Roller Rink floating out over it, mingling with the angry drone of the mosquitoes and muffled swearing from the other boats. A fistfight breaks out at the Evening In Paris. The sounds of sirens can be heard faintly in the Indiana blackness. It gets louder and then fades away. Tiny orange lights bob over the dance floor. . . .
>
> It's the drummer who sings. . . . When you've heard him over 2000 yards of soupy, oily water, filtered through fourteen billion feeding mosquitoes in the August heat, he is particularly juicy and ripe. . . .
>
> It is the sound of the American night. And to a twelve-year-old kid it is exciting beyond belief.

Are these memories really the stuff from which designs can be made?

From Memory to Design

A common thread links many of these landscapes. The aspects of the physical environment recalled as essentials are often elements outside the designer's palette. Can we design for the smell of freshly mown grass, frying chicken, or spring-moist soil, or for the sounds of crickets and spraying hoses, or for twilight, or the feel of the air on the first day of autumn? Many of the environmental cues noted are beyond the designer's control because of their nature, or because they are fortuitous or serendipitous interactions. This does not eliminate the possibility that remembered childhood landscapes can offer clues to more satisfying design, but it does not encourage it.

If indeed we recall experience more than environment, if the environment recalled is variable or of a scale, complexity, or character beyond the designer's control, can anything be gained from exploring the landscapes of memory further? If we seek simple and direct clues to design, probably not. If, however, we seek to learn more about how we experience the environment, both internal and external, and the pleasures we get from it, then several aspects of the landscapes of memory remain that might be explored.

Such exploration should avoid easy assumptions about the importance of such memories. A bias toward the importance of the environment or a fascination with evocative literary passages makes it easy to exaggerate the significance of environmental reminiscence. The usefulness of such memories is highly variable. As Florence Ladd has noted, "Environmental requirements are relative. They depend on an individual's culture, personal history, and perceptions of the range of environments available." But the acknowledgment is seldom honored in practice. Designers dwell on the satisfaction to be gained from the environment (possibly in reaction to their role in a society that does not reward design) and point out the importance of the environment to lower evolutionary forms, non-industrialized societies, and children. This is too often taken as implied proof that experiencing a satisfying physical environment is essential to all people, and that only a society as destructive as ours fails to recognize and act upon this fact. This is possible, but far from proven.

Still the conviction remains that these memories must have something to tell us—something as elusive as the dreams from which they come. Questions remain that we might ask, questions about the content of these memories, about the processes of forming and recalling them, and, primarily, about their role.

Are there universal forms embedded in these memories—unvarying symbols of the environmental experience? Although it is highly unlikely that universal human meanings are inherent in specific forms, some forms might be more susceptible to *receiving* such meaning. There are but a few universals of the human experience. The natural environment offers us sun, moon, storm, and fire. Certain simple forms, such as the circle, sphere, pyramid, cube, might be more "imageable" than others. Simple probability, requiring no resort to Jungian mysticism, might produce common combinations of form and meaning. Are there archetypes of form or space: pyramids, cubes, domes, caves, towers, and even sheltering gable roofs? The claims of the literature in this area are not convincing. Are there, if not archetypes of space, then archetypes of place: grove and plain, attic and cellar, nest and bridge? Are there persistent links between certain emotions and certain environments—archetypal behavior settings of internalized memory? Is the common association of that twilight front-yard time between children's supper and bed such a setting, or the exhilarating fear so often linked with empty streets, echoing late at night, that vision reminiscent of a De Chirico painting?

The literature of environmental archetypes seems not to progress but to repeat itself like a broken record. We do not need more articles reminding us that primitive dwellings have symbolic aspects, that up and down are not the same, or that here is not there, with predictable references to Jung, Bachelard, Eliade, Lord Raglan, and Clare Cooper Marcus. Each of these authors advanced intriguing hypotheses for speculation and even testing. Incestuous requotation has somehow transformed possibilities into established fact or revealed dogma, and does them a disservice, particularly since oblivion usually follows unexamined adulation.

The Role of Landscape Memory

How do our memories first form, lie stored, and then return? How far can we take Stegner's description of environmental pleasure determined by imprinting? Human beings are not ducklings. To say that predispositions toward the environment can be imprinted in humans at a certain stage of childhood is one thing, but to say that they must be is something else, and to say that they can only be determined then is something else again.

In later years what recalls those intensely felt landscapes? Particular environments or universal forms might stimulate recall—forms that might or might not derive from the original forms. The stimulus for recall might be wholly internal, bringing back memories with little need for environmental triggers. The recall of past environments might relate to the environment of the experienced present only at moments of conscious, intense recall, or it might operate subliminally. Maybe recall can be used consciously; maybe to be effective, it must be spontaneous and fortuitously cued.

What, finally, is the role of environmental memories in later life? If our concern is with memories of place, how they shape later pleasure, and the implications they might have for design, then the question of role is critical. If the testimony of writers is believed, these memories give a pleasure that, if sometimes bittersweet, is more intense and more active than simple environmental preference. But how are these memories used? Although we have no answers, we can speculate on possibilities.

One possibility, already mentioned, is most seductive to designers: that the environment of pleasure is imprinted permanently in childhood, and later recall shows simply a desire to experience again that pleasure of place, either the original place or one like it. If our attachment is only to the unique place once experienced, if there are no surrogates for the landscape of memories, then the environmental need calls for preservation and enhancement, not design. If such surrogates are possible, our task is extracting the essential elements for replication.

However, the association between recall or place and need for place might be less direct. Recall in later life might be associated with particular moods, needs, or states of mind or body. When we recall the comfort and security of childhood's twilight backyard, is it because of a desire for direct pleasurable environmental stimulus, or because we seek the emotion once associated with place? Adult recall might show not a simple desire for the pleasure of place but a need for the nurture and support experienced there. Does recall of place satisfy that need as well as actual return or replication of place?

What is critical might be the memory itself, as a memory. The pleasure of reminiscence might be just that—a pleasure independent of the environment experienced later, a pleasure in which the poignance and power come solely from internal play of memory, the very essence of the pleasure lying in the fact that it cannot be relived in the real world.

Memory's landscapes may hold no recipes for design—only questions with few answers. But the questions might be most useful as entry points to the varieties of environmental experience or as cues to further explorations. Consider two. Maybe the significance of memory's childhood places lies not in memory and childhood themselves but in directing our attention to two classes of meaningful landscapes: places for many stages or moods, and places created largely in the mind.

Consider that if writers have re-created their childhood places in their minds, they have created other places as well—places for old age, for example, or for support. Hemingway vividly portrayed such a setting in his story "A Clean, Well-Lighted Place," and Yeats envisioned his own haven for a mood or time of life:

I will arise and go now, and go to Innisfree,
And a small cabin build there, of clay and wattles made:
Nine bean-rows will I have there, a hive for the honey-bee;
And live alone in the bee-loud glade.

("The Lake Isle of Innisfree")

Consider, too, whether the memories of childhood place might loom large only because in later life we stop using the powerful ability to put ourselves into place and to create the mind's place. Edith Cobb comments that "it is significant that adult memories of childhood, even when nostalgic and romantic, seldom suggest the need to be a child but refer to a deep desire to renew the ability to perceive as a child and to participate with the whole bodily self in the forms, colors, and motions, the sights and sounds of the external world of nature and artifact."

Now it is common lore that childhood experience of place differs from adult experience and that the essence of the childhood experience is its directness and sensual immediacy. In *Topophilia* Yi-Fu Tuan explains: "The idea is that to a child nature is a feeling and an appetite. Once we reach the age of discernment thought places a veil, as it were, between nature and ourselves. Direct experience is edged aside by quiet appreciation. There is obvious truth in this belief." Maybe. Tuan is commenting on Wordsworth's "Tintern Abbey," but the same poet claimed:

My heart leaps up when I behold
     A rainbow in the sky:
So was it when my life began;
So is it now I am a man;
So be it when I shall grow old,
     Or let me die!

Fantasy

There is a lore among designers that the child's unthinking immersion in the environmental experience lies dormant but recapturable in the adult. But in focusing on that state of innocent immediacy, we ignore another ability of both child and adult—the ability to fantasize. Certainly fantasy plays a large role in memories of our childhood places. We have all returned to places we remember from our childhood only to find that our memory of them is mostly fantasy and that the physical image we perceive is now remarkably different and less powerful. Anthony Powell explores this experience in *A Dance to the Music of Time:*

> In my memory, the place had been larger, more forbidding, not so elaborately restored. In fact, I was far less impressed than formerly, even experiencing a certain feeling of disappointment. Memory, imagination, time, all building up on that brief visit, had left a magician's castle . . . weird and prodigious, peopled by beings impossible to relate to everyday life. Now, Stourwater seemed nearer to being an architectural abortion, a piece of monumental vulgarity.

And if fantasy plays a role in memory, if recall is a relative and active venture with fantasy, what of our childhood image when first constructed? In childhood, how much and how often did satisfaction depend upon fantasizing with the landscape? Introspective or literary examinations should tell us that fantasy was often an essential part of structuring close emotional ties to place. This active participation let Shepherd build a rich and stimulating place from the supposed ugliness and monotony of an Indiana mill town. Literary fantasy spurred Kazin to build in the streets of New York settings of a bygone day, an all-American environment removed from the Jewish streets of Brownsville, fantasy involving cultural as well as personal history:

> Every image I had of peace, of quiet shaded streets in some old small-town America I had seen dreaming over the ads in the *Saturday Evening Post,* now came back to me as that proud procession of awnings along the brownstones. I can never remember walking those last few blocks to the library; I seemed to float along the canvas tops. Here were the truly American streets; here was where they lived.

Fantasizing, or the creation of landscapes in the mind, might play a larger role in our interaction with the environment than we recognize or admit. What of that power to create internal landscapes? If memories serve best as memories, the internal fantasized landscape may have a vital role, too. It may not be just a reflection of an unsatisfactory real environment, but a landscape of its own with a power of its own. Perhaps remembered landscapes are simply one small subset of internal environments—one that we fall back on because the act of fantasizing environment has been socialized out of us. Perhaps Castaneda's hallucinogenic landscapes hold as much promise of pleasure as faint memories of nurseries and backyards at twilight.

We know so little about environmental recall and environmental fantasy that we must be careful in judging their value or attempting to use them. But we should not ignore the possibility that they give a sense of continuity to personal history and help us cope with the present. We might consider the role of recall and fantasy in the lives of old people.

Observation and common lore tell us things about the aging relevant to this question. The elderly are presumed, in life and literature, to spend much time reminiscing, living in their interior past, and retrieving intricately detailed memories of decades before while memories of more recent events become vague, confused, or lost. Tuan succinctly phrases another common belief when he states that "the environmentalist position works best when the human being is weak in some sense, as when he is an infant or senile, weakly or sick." Others suggest that the environment's effect on human behavior becomes greater as the competence of the individual decreases, as in the aging process. The aging are often housed institutionally in an environment both different from what they are accustomed to and also more uniform. This environment is less subject to their control but subject to considerable control by others. And the very term "nursing home" implies need for nurture—a state in which the landscapes of the memory or the mind may have increased significance.

Do landscapes of the mind play a particularly important role to the aging by fulfilling a function that the design of the physical environment should support or at least not impede? Or have the elderly partly solved their own problem? The mementos rescued from their lives—the favored vase, photo, or souvenir—may serve as better triggers to recall or fantasy of place than anything a designer could provide.

Some landscapes lie entirely in the mind. They might be landscapes of intense pleasure or terror made in varying degrees from memory or fantasy. There are also environmental pleasures in which internal structuring is minimal or irrelevant. But it might be useful to consider the fantastic shapes and colors of a drug experience and the fearful joy of a roller coaster as extremes on the same continuum of environmental gratification. On this continuum the poles of internal play and external stimuli, the present and the past, contribute in varying degrees.

Perhaps that is the lesson the designer can learn from the remembered landscapes of childhood—the reminder that every environmental experience draws on both the external and the internal landscape, both now and then. Many designers might admit to this proposition in the abstract, but few honor it in their design. The architects and landscape architects of the revival periods placed ruins in their landscapes not only as decorations or evidence of taste but as stimuli to literary fantasizing on the past and future, on the ambition and folly of mankind. Aalto is said to have faulted the Saarinens' Crow Island School for having no place for the lion to hide. Charles Moore makes explicit claims for the house as a repository of personal memories. But these are exceptions to a tradition that has considered the individual landscapes of the mind of little importance to design.

Nurturing Fantasy and Memory

Perhaps the lesson is not simply that past experiences predispose our preferences, but that internal recall and fantasy are active in every environmental experience and are often the essence of it. If so, environments should be designed to provoke those memories and fantasies.

How can such environments be designed? No one knows. The question returns us from the role of memory and fantasy to the process. We can only speculate on these processes, but it seems certain that if the designer has a role in manipulating cues, it will be a general one and not that of furnishing specific cues to trigger specific mental landscapes in specific people. This task is either impossible or so simple as to be within the control of the person involved with little need for a designer. The question is whether there are environments that encourage recall and fantasy. Is an environment rich in cues more likely to recall the pleasure of past or imagined places, or can recall or fantasy be encouraged by or sometimes depend upon a present environment that is neutral, malleable, or even hostile? Would cues be more effective if specific, or are they better left shadowy and ambiguous?

These questions now seem unanswerable. Maybe they always will be, despite the current fascination with the promises of neuroscience. The intricate synaptic pathways of the mind's memories and fantasies might forever elude our understanding, forever defy predictability in responding to environmental cues we provide. Maybe they are not answerable in generalities. Maybe there is no standard, given role for landscapes of memory or fantasy, but only roles that vary from culture to culture, from person to person, and from one moment to the next.

If the task of providing personal cues for internal landscape creation seems too complex for designers, we might comfort ourselves with the reminder that I have been dealing only with personal history. Perhaps the field of cultural memory and its attendant symbolism offer the real imperative and opportunity for designers. Observing the centrifugality and pluralism of contemporary culture, however, makes even that alternative seem less than comforting.

Our need is for more knowledge about the nature of environmental pleasure, and about that evocative, often used, but seldom examined term "place." Whether original place is substitutable or not, the fact that childhood memories might be precious to many of us gives us added incentive for preserving parts of the physical past—if not whole neighborhoods, at least reminders of past settings. We need provocative hints of the past ranging from the scale and complexity of Kevin Lynch's proposed historic collages to the sensitivity of the landscape designer who placed a large boulder to sit on where a childhood sandbox once rested.

Perhaps designers should join psychologists and neurologists in developing a high-tech environmental fantasy box where each of us, through electronic wizardry, can explore internally created landscapes. These landscapes could serve as guides for creating real settings. More prosaically, designers can help people explore their own sensitivities to place, help increase the power of people to manipulate their environment, and help preserve a larger-scale environment that is both diverse and organizable.

Meanwhile, we would do well to these keep literary landscapes in mind. Maybe poets have as much to tell us about environmental pleasure as research ever will. Then again maybe they haven't. But they are at least a pleasure to read.

◢ ◢ ◢ ◢   Around the House

I wish that May Watts were still alive to add another example to her chronological essay "The Fashionable House." We could use her wit and her eye
turned on the land of the McMansions. She would have loved the names.
Is there a developer's handbook suggesting references to Walter Scott's
novels—Kenilworth, Ivanhoe, glen, dale, etc.—or some species or land
use driven from the site or never there: Eagle Ridge, Quail Run, or anything Meadows or Farms, or at the top end Estates? So far, we have been
spared Estatelet, the obvious regional equivalent, after all, of Ranchette.
Retention basins are of course ponds, but swales and ditches offer more
leeway—brook, run, stream, creek, and branch (all originally regionally
specific terms) are qualifiers. No streets, please, just lanes, drives, courts,
and circles. A national newspaper recently noted that a new high-end development around a Jack Nicklaus golf course featured a cul-de-sac named
Golden Bear Court.

We know the houses, obviously meant as evidence of wealth and show.
(I prefer Nouveau Baronial to McMansion). Three garages of course. The
mailbox is enclosed in a big brick pier, ostentatiously expensive, looking secure enough to resist a nuclear attack. Landscape lore tells us that
Mediterranean-influenced cultures display their wealth in their residence
by hiding behind walls, while upscale houses in America surround themselves with land, the more the better. No more, for the Nouveau Baronial
does neither. Front-yard setbacks are often no greater than in lower-end
developments and side setbacks common to bungalows. Ringed around
a cul-de-sac, these houses remind me of the circus elephant parade, sans
music or rhythm. James Duncan once observed that in Westchester
County old wealth tended to hide their houses, while new money promi-
nently displayed them. Maybe Eagle Glen Estates is just the reductio ad
absurdum of that tendency, Walmartville instead of Westchester County.
But for sure, the house is the thing.

From Sacred Grove to Disney World: The Search for Garden Meaning

A garden is about nature.

The meaning of nature itself is a large issue, particularly for our time. Most of us assume that nature is inherently good for people and that it carries a universal meaning. Garden is seen as a special expression of that meaning. It has been an expression of importance in most cultures and the highest art form in some. It is an expression that, after several decades of being ignored by designers, has again become a focus of work, debate, and fashion.

Garden is a fuzzy and pluralistic concept. It includes three essential features: a thing grown (for pleasure or profit), the activity of growing (gardening), and a place (the garden). These total to a garden, whether a patch of tended vegetables or Vaux le Vicomte. What makes a garden a Garden, that carrier of meaning and high art form that concerns designers, is the intent to create an ideal environment, a place of special qualities, of itself or by allusion. Understood in this way, the garden is an intense and particular statement about our relations to nature, an archetypal statement of those relations.

It is not the only such statement. The idea of garden becomes clearer in contrast to other archetypal relations with nature. Hunting is one, an activity of long tradition, glorified in both cultural myths and modern meditations. Hunting as love of nature was a major theme in the works of that pioneer of contemporary environmentalism Aldo Leopold. No matter what one might think of it morally, hunting is a relationship that, at its purest, demands attention, involvement, dedication, knowledge, skill, and discipline in relation to nature.

Animism, too, is a distinct relation with nature, whether in the sense of assuming a soul within every organism or in the sense of that intense, transporting response to nature, distinct from the child's wonder or the adult's analysis. Animism is a relationship, not antithetical to the garden, but surely different, an emotion that can be experienced in the wild, or in a garden, or in any natural setting.

The wilderness experience, today a mystique, is another such relation. This immersion in "untouched nature," with its mystic and moralistic overtones, is as close to animism as contemporary secular society can come. Wilderness can be framed as polar to the garden, but that conceptual dichotomy does not take us far. But however one casts it, love (often distant love) of wilderness is a relationship with nature that has both similarities and differences with the garden, and a relationship that has a large, articulate following in American society. As such it has directly affected our attitude toward the garden.

Pastoralism shares with garden the vision of an ideal, harmonious relation with nature, in a setting affected by human presence. The difference is that in pastoralism human activity is but one element in an extrahuman or natural order. In a garden human intervention is the prime ordering element.

This essay is a simple and naive pursuit of meaning in the garden. My attention is mostly on the high garden, or at least the highly designed garden, where meaning is most sought, most expected. It is appropriate, then, to use simple, naive, and inclusive definition that can distinguish the garden from other relations with nature. For our purposes, a garden is an attempt to establish meaning by giving form to nature. This definition, if not better than several others that might be offered, fits the consensus about that elusive core of meaning and is particularly appropriate given the title of this volume. It adequately sets garden apart from the other archetypal relations and settings mentioned but does not distinguish the garden from the park or from some forms of environmental art. This non-trivial issue will be discussed later.

Themes in Garden Meaning

In our search for garden meaning the first question to ask is not what a garden *should* mean but what gardens *can* mean, what gardens *have* meant. A large catalog is at hand for answers, for the volume of literature on the pleasures of the garden probably equals those devoted to the parallel pleasures of the table and the bed, including illustrated, step-by-step instructions. (The parallels among garden design, cuisine, and sex—including the roles of creators, connoisseurs, and consumers—make a subject worth exploring.) Some years ago Nan Fairbrother laid out a sort of catalog of garden uses and delights: walking and talking and growing things; renewing jaded senses with multiple, ever-changing stimuli; providing seclusion for eating and playing games and making love; humanizing our geometric abstractions with the "background of green life";[1] giving to children the spur to fantasy and make-believe and to adults a glimpse of the sacred, the immortal, and the heavenly; and providing safe, harmless occupation for prisoners and women, a therapeutic pastime for invalids and the retired, and nostalgia for all. She saw the garden as a supportive and adaptable setting for many of our activities and our aspirations. In a practical approach to the difficult issue of meaning, she noted that gardening has always been thought of as exceptionally virtuous but adds, "I cannot see why growing flowers is a more virtuous way of spending time than taking opium, or any other selfish way of seeking happiness. But I can very well see that it is a more lasting pleasure, more socially acceptable, and certainly more healthy."

More than useful, more than delightful, the garden is often seen as a primal human setting. Along with, say, road or journey, shrine or temple, and home and hearth. Home and garden . . . both have origins combining the sacred and the domestic, and the garden is often seen as mediator or transition between home and hostile outer world, and both are fuzzy or pluralistic concepts, persistent but variable through time and across cultures.

The essence of garden, that core responsible for its persistence, is most commonly thought to be a spiritual-intellectual concept, an always mental, sometimes physical, artifact expressing humans' relation not only to nature but to their gods and their universe. This is what Genesis and generations of scholars have told us. Gardens have served as miniature re-creations of the cosmos, models of an ideal world made from the stuff of the real. From this comes the garden's importance and power. Others see it as a primary statement about a people's relation to work, family, and society. Some gardens, particularly those now overcome with tourists, can be understood as the ultimate expression of centralized power and vain caprice.

But whether its basis is social, spiritual, or psychological, the importance and persistence of the garden are not hard to understand. The garden is where we deal with the basic dialectic of our existence, the tension between life and death. Gardens, we know, are about life and ever-promised renewal, about dying. Americans are good at ignoring death but earlier ages needed no such reminders . . . death in Arcadia was clear to them. Sacheverell Sitwell saw in Italian gardens the ghosts of dead civilizations and told us it is death to fall asleep there. Siegfried Sassoon, musing over those same Italian gardens, also saw the ghosts of his poet predecessors seeing those same ancient ghosts.

When we build a garden, we exert control over those forces of birth, growth, decay, and death that in the end are beyond our control.[2] The impermanence of plants is not only the price but the validation of what we do. It reminds us that although our control passes, it is still control: control over not just clay or brick or steel, but over the stuff of life itself. This is why the hedges of a garden like Chateau de Beloeil are more than green walls, and why a vine-covered pergola is not a fragrant I-beam. To understand this essence of garden as manifest intervention in the processes of life and death, one might turn not to Versailles, as most writers suggest, but to bonsai, where the inevitable rhythms of nature have been slowed almost to a standstill.[3]

The garden not only expresses this, our most basic, dialectic, but layers upon it other dialectics: freedom/restraint, predictability/uncertainty, dominance/submission, nurture/neglect, order/disorder, variety/sameness, stability/change, and so on, even the tricky business of "garden as itself"/"garden as something else." Pruning as the counterpart of planting, the wait of the gardener who can choose what to plant but not what will survive, the loose drift of Jekyll's plantings through the geometric order of Luyten's walls and terraces—most intense garden experiences can be phrased as dialectics.

Nan Fairbrother set the garden apart from other art forms as the only one in which the basic elements are of intrinsic and complex interest in themselves. A plant is different from a brick or a tube of paint or a note on an oboe in three ways. It is a multisensory stimulus, it has a richly evident physical and visual structure exhibiting variety within order, and it contains many levels of information—from those of interest to the cell biologist to those simply wanting the cachet of a blue rose.[4] Wood and stone can be of intrinsic interest and structured complexity. Still, plants are commonly the foci of activity and interest in a garden, the reason for a garden's existence, while few but the obsessed architect or craftsman would consider a building's purpose to be the display of wood. However it might be explained, plants seem to be of inherent interest to humans.

But as designers we also know that a garden can be more than a collection of interesting natural elements; we know too that it can be a compelling spatial composition. As designers we also yearn for the return of those times when such compositions were even more than grand compositions, times when they carried meanings central to their society. J. B. Jackson read the garden as source of delight, work of art, and symbol, and Sun Xiao Xiang wrote of nature's garden, the artist's garden, and the poet's garden. It is this possibility of being appreciated on three levels, combined with the availability of so many potential dialectics, that makes the garden such a common collector of individual and collective meaning, and such a potent locus for symbols that exist across cultures and through history.

The American garden has become such a symbol of genteel respectability and banal cheer ("I count only the sunny hours") that we forget how frequently it has carried very different meanings. I have referred to the garden as a symbol of power, with its corollaries of order, ownership, class, and status, and as a symbol of sexuality, with its associated themes of love, sex, and sexism. Carole Fabricant reads the Georgian literary convention linking women and nature as a statement of then current realities concerning politics and property. Both woman and landscape were badges of male power and possession; both were to be artistically disciplined for public display but wantonly permissive for their owner's private delight.

Few designers today would admit to shaping their gardens as expressions of political and sexual dominance. Still, it is this general role of garden as powerful symbol complex that today's designers seem so eager to restore. However diverse their approach, their common slogan seems to be Robert Harbeson's aphorism "Gardens always mean something else."[5] Gardens have been a locus of meaning in many cultures, but not in modern America. Our "something else" got mislaid somewhere along the way. Before we rush to restore it, it might be helpful to inquire as to where it went, and why.

The Decline of the Garden

The decline of the garden as an important place carrying special meaning is not hard to understand. A complex of technological and social factors eliminated the necessity for domestic gardens, if not their desirability. The invention of the canning and later the freezing of vegetables; the use of speedy motor transport for the consumer and the producer-shipper of both flowers and vegetables; and the disappearance of the domestic carriage horse and other animals, with their useful wastes, all tended to make the domestic garden a discretionary space, not a necessary space. We are reminded at garden meetings that "statistics show that gardening is America's most popular outdoor activity" or some such statement. Maybe. But the popularity of gardening does not imply the continuity of the garden as a central social space dictating its own obligations and relationships any more than the popularity of television watching as our favorite indoor activity implies continuity of the family hearth.[6] The importance of the garden among immigrant and ethnic groups only highlights the decline of the garden as a work and social focus for most of us.

As the folk garden, a base for the high art, has declined in this century, so has that high form itself. The obvious absence of cheap skilled labor and the disappearance of the professional gardener in much of modern society seem too easily ignored in our current concern over bringing back garden meaning, although we are dramatically reminded when we see the decay of a Moghul showplace or Jekyll masterpiece. Lawn maintenance services with their mower- and sprayer-loaded pickup trucks have replaced the journeyman worker who was the central character of every English garden until World War II, just as the rental "plantscape" industry has replaced the gardeners and apprentices who once groomed the grounds of every elegant hotel. These restraints were better recognized decades ago by the pioneers of contemporary American landscape design, and in fact served as a major argument for their advocacy of a wholly new kind of "modern outdoor living." In the landscape, as in so many parts of modern life, speed and standardization have replaced patience and skill, and industry has replaced craft.

But it is debatable whether the garden as art or place of meaning has ever been much understood in America. Historically we have been a transient people addicted to movement, a condition that has shaped our taste in food, alcohol, and landscape . . . prized and promoted as our unequaled series of nature's marvels. David Lowenthal's 1968 characterization of the dominant images of the American landscape as size, wildness, and formlessness could well stand as a definition of anti-garden. Elbert Peets phrased it succinctly: "The current American is not a gardener . . . he does not care for plants as plants, though he loves grass, trees, sunlight and panoramic views as much as ever." The English bequeathed us a taste for lawns. We used them to unify our freestanding houses in one of the grandest developments of civic design that history shall know. But their taste for gardens seems not to have crossed the Atlantic. The guidebooks tell us that crowds make summer Sunday visits to Sissinghurst impossible. How many readers of the *New York Times* garden section have heard of Fletcher Steele or Russell Page, or could put a name to those familiar pictures of the Donnell Garden?

But if Americans, generally, have neglected the garden, there came a time when American designers actively turned against it. The relationship between the garden and the ascendancy of contemporary landscape design from revolution to establishment dogma is a complex subject, rife with ambivalence, crying for documentation, analysis, and interpretation. Reaction against the grip of tradition, particularly English tradition, on our landscape design and education can be traced in writings that began with Peets and continued for decades later. None of these writings attacked the garden per se: James Rose, for example, called for "freedom in the garden." For Peets, the enemy was the English informal landscape and its priesthood "wallowing in the pool of nature sentiment"; he explicitly extolled both the Italian formal garden and the folk garden. Rose dismissed the English landscape and concentrated his attack on the formal and axial Beaux-Arts tradition. Garrett Eckbo advocated larger areas of concern: the urban, rural, and primeval environments. Thomas Church and Rose addressed their first books to garden design and even included the word in their titles. Whatever their polemics for new models, new philosophies, and larger arenas for design, their real-world staple was the domestic garden; the Donnell Garden stands to American landscape design as the Villa Savoye does to International Style architecture. If by garden we mean an outdoor living space as an extension of the house, then the garden continued as the rock on which landscape architectural practice and education were based, a role equivalent to that of the single-family house in the rise of modern architecture.

But if by garden we mean the archetype of nature formed for meaning, if we mean the carrier of a culture's central symbols, it is hard to escape a sense of the garden's devaluation, a sense of it as the only available commission, executed in preparation for the awaited entry into the larger landscape and social relevance. Gardens were left unmentioned in the manifestos appearing just before World War II. Peets concentrated his hopes for the future on dams and stadiums, on "concrete mixers and steam shovels . . . booster energy and national highways." The course on garden design disappeared or was relegated to nonprofessional, community-oriented courses, the introductory site-design problem the "Smith Garden" became the "Smith Residence," and "plants" became "plant materials." Somehow the garden came to symbolize the dead hand of tradition, a rich man's toy, an emblem of social irrelevance or outright oppression. Can we imagine a postrevolutionary designer designing a space for outdoor living like Gatsby's, where in "blue gardens, men and girls came and went like moths, among the whisperings and the champagne and the stars"? In their search for larger scale, bigger issues, and greater impact, designers turned to models such as the TVA, parkways, and plans for river basins. Although this was a realistic and socially laudable redirection, we could also wonder whether a male-dominated profession thought that ladies grow flowers, but real men realign rivers.

The American landscape designers' rejection of the garden was supplemented by an earlier, broader, and more influential rejection, that of the mainstream European modern architectural tradition. The attitude of the classic modern architects to the landscape is an important subject just now beginning to receive the attention it deserves. It is a subject of great difficulty, because those attitudes were usually implicit, not explicit.[7] One undocumented and simple characterization can be offered: the classic modern tradition rejected the garden and enshrined the park. William Kent, we are told, leaped the wall and found all England a garden. The modern movement breached the city walls, dispersed the city itself, and envisioned all nature as a park. That park was an English landscape garden grown global and simple. The vision was buttressed by the nineteenth-century movements of social reform and municipal hygiene, and by the garden city. Nature was to be a healthy and utilitarian, but passive, redemptive setting. Visually it was to be as clean, simple, and uncluttered as modern buildings were, compared to their Victorian predecessors. It was to be a great pastoral sward upon which point blocks, borne by pilotis, rested as lightly as spaceships, as tastefully as cattle in a Repton Red Book. It was the vision of Ville Radieuse, of Roehampton, and of the high-style corporate office parks lining our freeways.

The difference between garden and park useful for this discussion is not one of scale, or user, or even necessarily uses, but of the role of nature.

The essence of garden is not only control of nature but demonstration of that control. Such demonstration is inessential, perhaps even distracting, in the park. The park lacks concentration on both the grown (the product of control) and the growing (the process of control).[8] This is a nontrivial difference, since many investigators comparing the two have contrasted the perceptions and motivations of park users with those of community gardeners. The park, as realized in the great Anglo-American visions of the nineteenth century, and in Ville Radieuse and classic modern architecture, conceptualizes nature as a benign and supportive environment conducive to moral activities and attitudes. This park is the idealized pastoral realized, a harmonious natural setting supporting and enhancing harmonious human activities. That the gardens of the nobility became the parks of the people is a reference not only to urban history but to designers' dreams. Control of nature is an end in itself in the garden, a means to human ends in the park. The garden art fails when it becomes so obviously contrived as to get in the way of meaning. The park fails when the benign becomes the bland, and no meaning at all is conveyed. That has been the fate of what began as a grand vision of modernism.

That vision, however, is still alive. It is a vision of optimism and liberalism, of friendly but too often banal nature. It is a vision that in a mindless form has pervaded our consciousness and our landscape. The landscape as debased park has produced a world we find troublesome and even threatening, a world so extensive that wild nature has become relief and haven. Garden become park, become landscape, has reversed the traditional relation of garden to wild. The wilderness has become an inverted, particularly American, *Hortus conclusus,* fenced off for the pack-framed pure of heart.

The Resurgence of Garden

The reasons for the resurgence of the garden might be as obvious, once articulated, as the reasons for its decline. First, we are seeing a reaction against the uniform, universal landscape of the classic moderns, for whom the preservation of global diversity was hardly a major worry. The international landscape has turned out to be not only pastoralized but homogenized. Whether this loss of diversity is real or simply a new, finer-grained pattern of diversity, self-conscious and nonregional, is a question I have discussed elsewhere and will only note here. Equally suspect is the common charge that the universal landscape produces "placelessness" now that "place" has become the catch phrase that "function" was to our predecessors. Garden styles have been as international and uniform (e.g., the bedding plants of British colonialism) as the building styles of European colonialism or workers' democracies. The garden is now seen as an antidote to the vaguely corporate, universal landscape that bores and bothers us. We could also view the return to the garden as one more manifestation of the privatization of our society, the garden replacing the park just as pool and patio replaced the porch. Is the garden as fitting a symbol of Reaganism as Greenbelt and then Columbia, both in Maryland, were for the naive confidence of the Roosevelt and then Kennedy-Johnson eras?

Simple cycles of fashion probably play a part in the resurgence of the garden as well. Among landscape architects, renewed interest in the garden might be seen as a predictable return to the historical, identity-bound core of the profession, redressing the imbalance attendant upon the expansion of social concerns and professional boundaries of the preceding two decades. Architects and the architectural press have also been conspicuous in the return to the garden, and simple architectural conceit might explain much of their attention and rhetoric. From the earliest examples of the English landscape style through both European and American classic modern architecture, from Rousham House through Villa Savoye to the Donnell Garden and the Farnsworth House, the organizing geometry of the house stopped at its walls. Architects' recent fascination with the garden might have been forecast as part of the recurring cycle of building retreat and then advance in the continuing naturalist versus formalist landscape debate. Current design rhetoric is similar to that of the two great turn-of-the-century protagonists of the formal garden, when Reginald Blomfield and George Sitwell faulted the English landscape style that had dominated eighteenth- and nineteenth-century garden design for its failure to relate the landscape to the house it served. The comparison hardly justifies some contemporary architectural silliness, but it provides a respectable precedent for the garden grids of Charles Moore and Barbara Stauffacher Solomon. It is fun, if unprofitable, to speculate whether the impact of Moore's clever, articulate writings and Solomon's gorgeous graphics played any part in the renewed prominence of gardens in landscape architectural publishing. What matters is that designers are back in the garden, forming nature and seeking meaning.

The Search for Meaning: Problems

There are many problems, some obvious but some less so, in restoring garden meaning, obstacles to once again centering powerful and accepted symbolism on the garden. Many of these result from new attitudes toward nature. Control over nature, the essence of garden meaning, has become so commonplace as to mean little. Eight decades have passed since Peets looked to vast highway systems and dams for the act of dramatically molding nature. Those demonstrations first became routine, and then commonly questioned for their environmental effects and philosophy. The Victorian era was the last great age of gardens in the European tradition. There might be no generalizable answer to the question of why one culture places profound meaning on plants and gardens and why another does not, but we can see how many aspects of Victorian society make their predilection understandable. The Victorians reveled in technological process and virtuosity, much of it centered on construction and environmental control. Improved, less expensive glass production and cast-iron framing, and advances in economical, easily available heating and hydraulic systems in artifacts ranging from Wardian cases to huge conservatories, when combined with the English love of plants and gardening, opened new worlds of botanical control and display. If we add to that the imperialist sweep of exploration, colonization, and collecting, then the Victorian preoccupation with gardens (and zoos) as social focus and value carrier seems not only logical but almost inevitable.

No such obvious technological and social synergism advances the role of the garden today. Our technological advances and our fascination are focused on personal and portable electronic wonders relating little to mastery of the natural environment (although much to the way we enjoy that environment), advances beyond the intuitive understanding that could comprehend, but still wonder at, the conservatory at Chatsworth.[9] Easy acceptance of, and then growing dismay over, our power to rework nature, combined with a traditional American preference for remote and spectacular grandeur, have redirected our search for symbolic nature from the garden to the wilderness.

What we ask of nature, and how we use it, have changed as well. Electronics and personal transportation have produced new ways of enjoying the natural world. We emphasize motion and activity, individual transitory experience, often heightened by sophisticated technology. Our mobility and technology allow us not only to see many places briefly, instead of lingering in and deeply understanding only one, but to experience nature in new ways. Dirt biking, hang gliding, and surfing, often abetted by iTunes, emphasize not lingering or traditional social meanings but brief, intense, individual sensate experience, often tinged with risk or even danger. Jackson characterized this new relation with nature as "the abstract world of the hot-rodder." I call it the high-tech, hedonistic quick fix. Whatever we have gained, we have lost the taste for those quiet times of contemplation central to the experience of so many older gardens.

Shared symbolism, so central to the high art of the garden, is also a difficult problem for our time. The attempts of modern designers to achieve it show a history of failures, from Mies's steel-on-concrete-on-steel corners, through Venturi's gilded antenna, to Moore's plated capitals. The symbols that have empowered great architecture and great garden art are what Mary Douglas called condensed symbols, symbols that carry not just one meaning but an accretion of many meanings, layered upon each other over time. They are symbols that are commonly agreed upon, not designer chosen; that connote deep affective meaning, not quick cleverness; and that are integral to a context that is culturally agreed upon as appropriate. Are there such symbols for our time, or do we lack them, at least as they are capable of being expressed in physical design, altogether? Amos Rapoport has suggested that such powerful symbols as we have are more likely to be individual than communal. This seems plausible for a culture as centrifugal, as pluralistic, as individualistic, and as privatized as ours. A lack of shared symbolism does not rule out the garden as a carrier of powerful meaning, but it does discount the likelihood of meanings that speak strongly to the whole society.

The Search for Meaning: A Program

Where might such meaning come from? How might we build into our gardens a symbolic content to match that resurgence of design interest among designers? Such meaning can come only from a careful, serious assemblage of scholarship, research, and design, a complex of work that follows a program, not a fashionable whim. Our scholarship should analyze, synthesize, and interpret garden history in order to pose questions for research. Our research should pose and test hypotheses that might help answer those questions. Our design should both apply the results of our research and serve as a laboratory for it, a circular, not linear process.

Scholarship

The scholarship that will help us is a far cry from the current deluge of picture books and from the model of garden history that delves ever more deeply and narrowly into archival minutiae. We need interpretive and rigorous exploration that goes beyond the garden and its great designers to explore the relation of garden design to its political, social, economic, and technological context. Many histories and a few journal articles offer token recognition and simplistic, timeworn generalizations on these topics, but few take it as their central concern. Those works that deal seriously with garden meaning in history relate it to its sister arts and intellectual simplifications about the "spirit of an age." One does not need to be a Marxist, or even a cultural materialist, to realize that ideas do not arise completely independently of the economic and social matrix of their time. Carole Fabricant and Robert Williams have broadened our understanding of the social, economic, and political context of the Georgian garden. Nicolette Scourse's book on Victorian flowers is a model for comprehensive, integrated treatment of the social, economic, and technological setting upon which garden art is based. Such studies will provide no easy answers for contemporary design. The scholarship we need will not tell us what a garden means or what a garden should mean. It can suggest why gardens were or were not a locus of meaning at particular times and why and how that meaning emerged from the society that produced it. Such work will serve as a catalyst for designers, a stimulus to thinking seriously and reflectively about meaning, a standard against which a designer's clarity and explicitness about assumed meaning and its relation to society can be measured.

Research

A world of potential research into garden meaning lies before us, a world as yet hardly explored, let alone mapped. The traditional literature is filled with assumptions about the satisfactions gained from gardens and gardening. These assumptions are often phrased in syrupy language, but are at least explicit. One musing by Nan Fairbrother, "Why Men Have Gardened," in her book *Men and Gardens,* alone contains enough clear and succinct statements about gardening, as both an activity and a place, to keep researchers busy for years. Environmental psychology possesses a repertoire of potentially useful concepts for structuring and exploring these hypotheses: competency theory, cognitive structuring, information processing, play theory, and so on. Environmental psychologists have laid out clear exemplars for the larger world of satisfaction from nature in general. While less has been done for the smaller, more intense world of the garden, Fairbrother's description of gardening as a tranquil occupation, "busying the mind with quietness," brings to mind Rachel Kaplan and Stephen Kaplan's concept of involuntary attention. Yeats's classic statement of the pastoral garden, "The Lake Isle of Innisfree," bears on the psychologist's exploration of nature as stimulus and the concept of restorative environment. What psychological concepts or processes might help us understand or better categorize Sun's intuitive concept, referred to earlier, of nature's garden, the artist's garden, and the poet's garden? The testing of traditionally assumed garden satisfactions with the concepts and techniques of environmental psychology is a research direction as fruitful as it is obvious. That it has hardly been suggested tells us much about the superficial thinking of designers and the constantly lamented gap between designers and social scientists.

Design Approaches

Meaning in the garden, that response beyond the sensory and pictorial, that essence of the poet's garden, has never been confined within the garden itself. Garden meaning has been shared with other art forms and landscape forms. Some designers are conducting their own search for meaning without waiting for the scholarship or research of others. They are searching both inside and outside the garden.

Designers are turning to several sources for help in this search for meaning. Contemporary high art, with its postmodern philosophies and forms, is one of these. This is reasonable; the link between the garden and other art forms, particularly sculpture, is traditional. Almost any contemporary high-style garden is sure to contain a piece of equally modern sculpture, but integration of garden and art is more than the obligatory gesture toward sculpture, more than pastoral plop art. Martha Schwartz and Ian Hamilton Finlay have, in different ways, moved beyond the garden as a green backdrop for isolated sculptures to serious explorations into the synthesis of sculpture and garden. Even the most thoughtful synthesis of contemporary plastic and garden arts, however, poses a problem. The tenets and vocabulary of contemporary art are not shared among the wider society. A simple fact—probably regrettable, but surely true. The problem is not elitism. The latter is a charge often flung at garden designers by the too few socially conscious designer-activists; it is a charge that mainstream designers seem proud to accept. The function of art, after all, is to lead public taste, not to pander to it. But the proper definition of elitism is rule or domination by a powerful clique, by the best and the brightest. Leadership is fine. But if designers are to accept the charge of elite leadership, they should look back once in a while to see whether anyone is following. Contemporary art and avant-garde design are not elitist, but arcane. The problem today is compounded by the fact that by the time a style is understood and absorbed by a wider public, the designers have moved on to other publication-rewarded themes. These remarks are simplistic, but we ignore such simple reminders constantly. These difficulties do not negate the potential of a contemporary garden/high art synthesis, which can and will be a powerful experience. They do sketch out limitations. The problem is similar to that of gardens based on personal symbolism: meaning is shared by few, not many. The difference is that in a garden built on personal symbolism we do not know who will share the meanings. (A research program such as I have outlined would, however, provide clues.) In a high-art garden we do know who will share meaning: the designers' peers and readers of the arts literature. The argument that shock is good for you might be valid, but certainly not sufficient. Shock might prepare one for meaning; it does not produce it. (That tenet of some other contemporary architectural gardens, that schlock is good for you, need not be taken seriously.)

Earth art, a clumsy term covering the work of diverse environmental artists using natural materials and phenomena, shares many of the beliefs and vocabularies of the garden as high art. For our exploration of garden meaning, however, it can be better understood as being opposite. If the high-art approach conveys meaning to a small subculture, earth art attempts to convey universal meanings. It is precultural in its return to immediate sensations and the primal awe of experiencing nature and its transformations, those feelings thought to be universal from our beginnings as hominids. It is an attempt to reanimate our art with the power of the sacred grove.[10] In a pre-garden society, however, awe and symbolism were constants in the human-nature relationship. The great archetypal environmental artworks—Stonehenge, Avebury, Silbury Hill—did not create that awe; they focused and celebrated it. Current earthworks are not foci amid such continuity, but isolated incidents in a culture bent on different ends. The distance between our sophistication and the naïveté Henry Adams found in the Virgin worship of Chartres is as nothing compared to the distance between us and the builders of Silbury. Can that kind of wonder and meaning sought by so many of the artists of our time and others move beyond the transient experience, even survive, in a culture that is at best indifferent to it? The radical feminists who seek to establish religious ritual around Mother Earth's moundings seem to be the only ones exploring this potential.

The power of many contemporary earthworks is formidable. Are they gardens? More pertinently, do they fulfill the role of gardens? If any work of art that forms nature to provide meaning is a garden, then they are gardens. If gardens are expected to move beyond primal response and offer accretion of layered meanings predictably shared among a wide audience, the answer is problematic. Earth art is best understood as a pre-garden, an attempt to short-circuit all the centuries of shared symbolism turned empty, to return to the time when nature was Garden, maybe slowly to build again to nature as garden.

Other designers have turned to a very different reference in their search for meaning—the regional landscape. Warren Byrd's designs are based on the evolving landscape of tidewater Virginia, and Terry Harkness's on the agricultural landscape of central Illinois. Scholars are only beginning to explore the relationship between agriculture and the birth of garden art. What we do know is that the larger landscape, both cultural and natural, has been at the base of some great garden styles. The Chinese tradition is the epitome. It was the result of layer upon layer of abstractions of the larger landscape: from landscape, to landscape myth, to landscape poem and painting, to garden. It would take years to move from Byrd's and Harkness's start to that kind of art (years being the electronic age equivalent of earlier dynasties), but the possibility is there. The meaning source here is widely accessible; if it is limited by region, it cuts across lines of class and taste. The connoisseurs of silos and hedgerows probably outnumber the connoisseurs of New York art, at least in central

Illinois. Their lore is accessible, if one is willing to substitute a trip to the courthouse café for an evening with the *New York Review of Books*.

One last and provocative approach to garden meaning is worth exploring. We can see it in the work of Bernard Lassus, the most innovative garden thinker of our time. Lassus seeks to rebuild garden meaning by turning not to sources beyond the garden, or before the garden, but to the essence of garden itself. He sees this essence as the contrast between the knowable and the illimitable, between the mappable and tangible world of the garden and the terra incognita of the world outside the garden. In his view the failure of garden meaning in our time comes from the fact that our entire planet is now not only knowable but known. There are no blank places on our maps or in our minds, no heres where there could be dragons. To Lassus the power of garden depends on the power of its opposite. His gardens become true gardens again because he supplies that illimitable. Our horizontal world is too well known, so Lassus provides us with the vertical: bottomless voids into which dropped pebbles travel forever. He builds caverns for us and engulfed villages that are seen and then vanish, and giant insects emerging from the water. The artifice of Lassus would destroy our complacency by providing uncontrolled nature. He brings back fear of nature, to the benefit of the garden. (Maybe along with fear, we should bring back sex, which also seems to have been missing from the garden for too long.) If his conceptual approach is unique, Lassus also stands almost alone among contemporary designers in welcoming technology in the service of experience. He uses it to hint at fear, at the tingle of the beyond and the awesome upon which the older vision of the sublime rested, and he has managed to incorporate at least a hint of such fantasies and references into built work. What a garden a team of Lassus, Vicino Orsini, and the technical wizards of Disney might have made!

Lassus also explicitly brings fantasy back to the garden. It has never been gone, just ignored. Or maybe it has just looked at from the wrong end. Gardens are commonly thought of as fantasy concretized. At its most serious this view sees the garden as a prime, tangible expression of a culture's most powerful fantasy—its worldview. At the other extreme the garden is seen as the place to indulge in the concretization of fantasy turned fluff. Architecture is serious business in this view, but the garden is where we can build our whimsy. It is significant that Charles Moore, about the only American architect of our time who unashamedly deals with fantasy and whimsy, is leading the architects' march back to the garden. The trip to concretized fantasy is a dangerous one. Moore's discipline and intelligence keep his work this side of silliness. When such checks are removed, we get Stanley Tigerman's terminally cute topiary. But the garden can be seen as, not a concretization of fantasy, but a spur to fantasy. The Georgian Arcady was a fantasy cue for the cognoscenti. Disney World is a concretized fantasy, but can we doubt that much of its popularity lies not in the literary fantasies it programs but in the internal fantasies it releases, fantasies that are, in the jargon, both interactive and open-ended?

The garden deals with death, but a second hallmark distinguishes it from architecture. The garden is the unprogrammed space par excellence, the space that serves the dwellers' unpredictable, internal activity, not designer-codified external activity. Its power to generate fantasy, both shared and individual, lies in the fact that it is an artificial place made from the stuff of the real. It is real enough to be convincing, but not so real as to constrain the unreal. That is a powerful form of meaning, or the means to it.

Our search for garden meaning raises the problem, already alluded to, of audience. When a garden speaks of meaning shared by a wide community, several things happen. Most simply, satisfaction is gained by more people, as it should be in a democratic society. Beyond that, it allows communal sharing and hence reinforcement and enhancement of those joys. The garden is linked to cultural values, social forms, and the other arts, reinforcing them and in turn being reinforced. Lastly, it ensures its own survival by receiving social approval, by becoming important. Survival does not ensure quality but it is a prerequisite for its development. Gardens need consumers. Garden meaning requires more than an adequately broad audience. It requires connoisseurship. Meaning and connoisseurship are inextricably linked. A critical mass of critics, an informed, articulate group of garden participants and patrons, enriches garden meaning and art in two ways. First, it demands ever more perfection and innovation in the garden and rewards the designer who provides them. Second, such patronage permits accretion, the building of meaning upon meaning. This accretion is a mark of great and enduring art forms. It rewards understanding with joy at many levels, from the sensory to the cerebral, from the literal to the abstract.

Connoisseurship requires a specialized literacy. The literalness required of a garden is in inverse proportion to the literacy of its audience. The long decline in the English garden from Georgian to Victorian times can be read as the withering of connoisseurship and the rise of consumerism. The greatness of the Chinese garden can be read as a long progression from the literalness of the landscape as itself to the layered references and abstraction of the Wang Shih as landscape of the mind. This is a way to understand both the problem and the potential of Byrd's and Harkness's gardens. One or two gardens will be interesting, but if too literal in their references they will soon lose their return and be discovered once and for all. To test their potential we need many of them, with varying referents and with interplay between varying levels of abstraction from those referents. Connoisseurs' demands for ever more complex and intricate abstract relationships can corrupt a style as surely as descent into literalness in the service of sentiment. It will be a long time before we need face those worries, however. Garden connoisseurship has died just as has the garden craft. George Sitwell's century-old book-length musing on gardens was the last of that tradition, its zenith, its climax. To read it is to understand the height of intellectual power and emotional richness that connoisseurship reached, is to understand the critical role of the classical education and the grand tour upon which that connoisseurship rested, is to understand the loss we have suffered. Rebuilding garden connoisseurship will be even more difficult than rediscovering the garden craft. Whether the short cycles and intense media exploitation of the contemporary design world will hinder or help its development is problematic. So is the question of which comes first, consumers or connoisseurs. What is certain is that we need both.

In Conclusion

A few simple rules will help in our search for meaning. We should remember that we live in a diverse, pluralistic culture in which widely agreed upon meaning and powerful accepted symbols are the exception. Because of this we need to be explicit about what meanings we hope to convey, and why, and to whom. We need to identify explicitly our consumers and our connoisseurs and to distinguish between them.

We should acknowledge technology, not flee from it. There is no more reason for us to ignore computers and holograms, light shows and lasers, in our gardens than there was for the Victorians to ignore hydraulic and heating technologies in theirs.

We should remember that a garden is not a building and to emphasize the difference. A garden is about birth but equally about dying. Its power depends upon this. A garden is not just a fragrant piece of architecture. A garden is about fantasy. A garden can be not only a fantasy realized but a fantasy provoked.

We should accept that this is a time of exploration, not consolidation. We might even rejoice in that fact. But exploration is not aimless wandering. We need to think and to reflect, and to avoid the symbols sweepstakes. Our scholarship should shape our research, our research should shape our design. But that is not enough. If we need research in the service of design, we can also exploit design in the service of research. Each of our garden designs could pose a hypothesis and a plan to test it. That is the difference between exploration and wandering.

The path to contemporary garden meaning will be a hard one, as lined with cul-de-sacs, contrived vistas, and artifice as the garden itself. It is a path worth taking. It is a path that will bring disappointments as well as pleasures. We do not know where it will lead us. That is as it should be and as it must be. As Don Juan has told us, there are no destinations. There are only journeys.

Notes

This essay is based in large part upon a study supported by a National Endowment for the Arts Fellowship. I am also grateful to Anne Whiston Spirn for her many perceptive comments, questions, and suggestions.

1. It is not obvious how a nonhuman material "humanizes" an environment, or why certain nonhuman materials, such as plants, are thought to accomplish this while others, like rats or weeds or bugs, do not. Maybe Fairbrother is using a concept sloppily, just as architects prattle endlessly about "human scale." But she is expressing a common belief and one worthy of research.

2. Steven Kaplan (1983) distinguishes among three related concepts often subsumed under the term "control" in peoples' relation to the environment. These are the assurance of non-randomness, or things being "under control"; participation, or things being "not beyond one's control"; and effective personal power, or being "in control." All three help in understanding the diverse meanings of a garden.

3. This definition of the garden as control over nature for human pleasure is useful and concise but raises some perplexing questions. By nature do we mean living nature or will rock and water do? Does control include imitation of the natural by the artificial? Is an atrium filled with plastic plants a garden? Does control ultimately include total banishment? There are no plants in Ryoan-ji but we call it a garden. Is it a garden because of its relation to the trees visible beyond? Is it a garden because its rocks and gravel refer to nature? Is it then not a garden or is it the final garden, a reductionist key to the ultimate garden in and of the mind?

4. When we refer to the basic garden element we assume plants are meant. Karel Capek, the Czech author best known for coining the word "robot," has written a witty, dissenting essay in which he suggests that the richest and most fascinating element in the garden is not the plant but the soil, and provides a catalog of its attractions.

5. This is a quotation as common these days as Bacon's reference to the Lord God and the first garden once was, and just about as useful for actual garden design work.

6. I will leave for others the question of whether the "yard" or "lawn" (terms etymologically distinct but almost interchangeable in contemporary usage), so important in the American environment, should be considered a garden.

7. Frank Lloyd Wright and the European modernists represent polar approaches to the building-landscape relation, but there were also distinct visions within the European tradition itself. Alvar Aalto surely would have to be distinguished from the so-called International Style mainstream. Even within the latter, Le Corbusier and Hilberseimer held different ideas of the role of nature and the landscape.

8. This distinction between park and garden, based on demonstration of control, like the earlier definition of garden based upon exertion of control, is handy and concise but not watertight. Where, for example, does a "garden" by A. E. Bye fall under such a dichotomy? And how do we deal with Sylvia Crowe's contention that the royal hunting park was one of the two archetypes for the concept of garden?

9. The reductio ad absurdum of computerized, electronic miniaturization of nature will be a solar-powered Japanese wristwatch garden, custom programmable for owner-chosen displays of growth and seasonal change and imported by Hammacher Schlemmer.

10. The sacred grove and Disney World can serve as antipodal limits to the garden, and to human relations with nature, in several ways: as pre-garden versus postgarden, or as the primacy of meaning versus its trivialization, or as nature's magic versus human technology masquerading as nature's magic.

♪ ♪ ♪ ♪ On Criticism

We tell one another that the profession of landscape architecture needs more design criticism. Not just more of the familiar internecine pronouncements about intellectual inadequacy or social irresponsibility, but critical evaluation of actual design work, built or even unbuilt. Not just contentions about design, but criticism of designs. It is beginning to happen. From some mild forays by distinguished critics in *Landscape Architecture* magazine through *Harvard Design Magazine* and *Land Forum* to the series of critiques from Louisiana State University, criticism, if scarce, is at least with us. Before we suffer the pains of getting what we've asked for, let us stop a minute and be sure we know why we want criticism—for what, by whom.

Well, damn! Theater and books and art and music and, now, even architecture, they all have it, don't they? Doesn't landscape architecture need it too? To be sure, criticism is a marker of being taken seriously, of being worthy of note—hopefully by others, certainly by ourselves.

The current state of architectural criticism raises both skepticism and hope. The relation between professional critics and designers seems ambivalent and even incestuous, and the critics bear most of the responsibility for the decreasing half-life of reputations and the accelerating cycles of formal fashion. On the plus side, architectural writers have called attention to important issues of criticism: social context or formal and visual character, designer's intent or actual impact and effect, the spectacular versus the plain but socially responsive—and so on. Still, criticism is unlikely to produce any immediate improvement in social conscience, program, design skills, or quality of materials and workmanship (read "project budget").

Criticism can, however, make two obvious if indirect contributions. It can encourage debate, a basic requirement for jacking up the level of our discourse. Cycles of honest comment and rebuttal promote clarity and explicitness, both in defining positions and in defending the designs based upon them—generously assuming that indeed there is a relationship between rhetoric and results. This type of criticism both advances theory and is fed by it, and theory is sadly lacking in our field.

The second role for criticism is the building of an informed and more demanding audience—landscape connoisseurs, if you will, stripping that term of its preciousness. Public concern about landscape is now manifested in generally negative responses: chronic unease over sprawl and acute protests about change in neighborhoods or about anything remotely historical. Lay-oriented criticism is surely necessary, if maybe not sufficient, for developing a broader public concern—a demand for richer landscapes as well as some idea of what makes such landscapes.

Can the same mode of criticism promote both goals? Not quite. Conversation within the discipline and that with the public entail different scales of time and text, different outlets, and, apparently, even different prose skills. Communication with a public rewards clear, forceful, even elegant writing, traits commonly thought incompatible with tenure seeking or design conferences. But if the roots of the criticism differ, the issues must be common. And by issues I mean all the issues, from the most abstract to the most immediate, from the relationship of design to corporate capitalist culture to that of riser to tread.

Most current architectural and landscape criticism and almost all academic criticism aim at positioning design in cultural context. They focus on the relationship between a design and the system it serves. Another frequent approach is the designer's intent. This intent, whether phrased in project rhetoric or inferred by the critic, is compared to the completed project as perceived by the critic. Both of these approaches yield a wide range of critical opinion: Compare jury remarks about an American Society of Landscape Architects President's or Honor Award, say, and the subsequent—and virtually inevitable—academic assaults on the same project. In contrast to criticism aimed at a lay audience, this professional criticism emphasizes context more than experience, intent more than user reception. Premise counts for more than experience. I am not suggesting that concerns about context and intent are unimportant, merely that the imbalance needs to be redressed—not reversed—for a complete and effective criticism.

This effective criticism is not a matter of dumbing down, of treating craft instead of intellectual content. Any serious reader of lay criticism is as capable of understanding the landscape import of Heidegger or Derrida as are those designer/academics who exhibit intellectual Deleuzions of grandeur—and who probably struggled to pull a B– in Philosophy 101. Experiencing a landscape as ephemeral and varying need not be the end of criticism, but it should surely be the beginning. That moving from the experienced to the abstract, from the immediate to the intellectual, from the sensory to the speculative is probably what made J. B. Jackson the most influential landscape critic of our time.

Moreover, beginning with the experience allows us to push beyond that hermetic self-referential world of text and two-dimensional images that has become the currency of our education, debate, criticism, and judgment, a world of publications in which too often text and graphics don't even relate to each other, let alone to the landscape itself.

Achieving a more complete criticism shouldn't be that hard. Ironically, it is the kind of explication, discussion, and judgment that fills the buses and bars at any conference—a critical microcosm, articulate and impassioned, of contention about textures, context, workmanship, form, social equity, access, and design philosophies all blended together. We need to preserve some of that mix in print.

◢ ◢ ◢ ◢ The Camaro in the Pasture

The countryside just doesn't look like countryside is supposed to anymore. The ax, plow, horse, and rifle have long been displaced by the mobile home, propane tank, satellite dish, and pickup. The tractor-tire garden out front is now an eight-year-old Camaro with a "for sale" sign on it. The changes include conversion of farmland to residences or for urban expansion, soil erosion and siltation, corporate farming (whatever that is), the draining and development of wetlands, and the proliferation of suburbia and second-home mania. The new rural landscape is a creature of the petrochemical revolution, the internal combustion engine (whether in tractor or automobile), universal electrical power, and universal electronic communications. The agricultural system and the agricultural landscape have changed. New crops have been introduced and regional crop patterns have changed. Productivity on some land rises while marginal land is abandoned. People continue to emigrate from rural areas in most parts of the United States.

Although we expect change and we claim to accept it, something about this change seems qualitatively and quantitatively different: the "countryside" seems to be disappearing. Our response has been to attempt to slow change, or at least guide it. This usually takes some form of containing or concealing change to leave the look of what's "always" been there.

That older landscape was not just a physical, social, and economic phenomenon. It was a conceptual image, an unexamined, shared vision of the countryside. It was economically, socially, and visually organized around people living on the land and earning a living from the land, particularly through agriculture and some extractive land uses. Few people lived on the land who didn't earn a living from the land. It had a basic conceptual and hierarchical organization—city, town, village, hamlet, freestanding farmstead, and, finally, wild land. Economically, it was organized hierarchically and centrally as well, with functions and markets linked to settlements. Whether our vision of it was as sweet and nostalgic as that of Laura Ingalls Wilder or as ribald and offbeat as that of Carolyn Chute, it was a shared vision. Ironically, forces changing our countryside seem to have produced a nostalgic backlash that perpetuates the image. Remember Wilder's *Little House on the Prairie* books, and the Walton family flashing across millions of television screens?

But more than agriculture is changing out there. A new landscape is just around the corner. The new landscape has a different purpose. It will work differently, and it will look different.

The landscape was never as simple as its image. Hugh Raup has described the changes and cycles that one New England landscape has gone through. Another interpretive summary of the new landscape is John Louv's phrase "buckshot urbanization." Peirce Lewis coined the term Galactic City to describe a new urban form of city that can't be understood at all in terms of the old city, but only in terms of itself, and noted its expansion into the countryside.

The new old rural landscape was a place where people worked on the land, earned their living on the land, and lived on that land. The new rural landscape is a residence and occasional workplace for people whose livelihood depends not at all upon the land.

Perhaps our landscape is undergoing a paradigm shift unprecedented since the rise of agriculture or of urbanism. The humanized nonurban landscape, throughout human history, has been almost completely shaped by people who worked and lived on that land (or, sometimes, by people who owned the land and by workers who lived off its profits). The new nonurban landscape, at least in the United States, is being shaped largely by people to whom the rural landscape is nothing more or nothing less than an alternative residential location. Whether they be commuters, retirees, or desktop publishers earning a living from their den, they regard the rural landscape not as a productive system or a way of life but as a locational amenity.

Just as this is a new landscape being shaped by new forces, we increasingly find that institutions developed in the old landscape are inadequate or irrelevant in the new. For example, traditional forms of political organizations, as Louv and others have pointed out, are giving way to privatized systems—the county sheriff, for example, is being replaced or supplemented by private security systems, chain-link fences, and dogs. Another example is the fact that so many landscape architects pin their hopes for guiding and shaping this new countryside on the Soil Conservation Service, an institution that was, in fact, developed to solve very different problems in very different landscape systems.

Traditional concepts of city, town, village, hamlet, farmstead, and wild have little relevance to this new landscape and this new way of life. As Peirce Lewis observed, our habit of constantly trying to interpret the new landscape in terms of the old one is futile and actively hinders understanding. The new landscape is one in which traditional concepts of central place and hierarchical organization are meaningless. It is a landscape, again in Louv's phrase, of buckshot urbanization.

As designers, our major concern has not been in developing a new vision for a new landscape, but in saving the old. I do not say that the old is not worth saving. I do worry about the fact that it seems most of us have focused our thoughts on how we can accommodate some sort of change without destroying the visual character of the existing countryside, and paid little attention to what the new landscape wants to be.

If the essence of the new countryside is as different as I think it is, and the forces developing it as powerful as they seem, how likely is it that we can somehow hide it, fit it in where it cannot be seen, confine it to nonproductive farmland, or in any other way sweep it under the rug? Not likely.

Let me suggest a way of looking at the new and the old that might give us a little more intellectual, creative, and professional freedom. We tend to see the new landscape, in relation to the old, as seeping out of the city along the interstates and invading the weakest chinks of the old landscape, as if it were some disease. A more productive way of looking at the new and the old landscapes might be as made from two distinct patterns.

The traditional countryside can be understood in terms of sophisticated regional science or central place theory, theories of agricultural land use and rent, and so forth. Much of it is framed in the Jeffersonian grid, the most powerful human abstraction ever laid on the land. Think of the new landscape as based on entirely different motivations, economics, and sociology. It is a pattern with many fewer spatial and distance restrictions than the old network and, in fact, with electronic communications, about as a-spatial as any spatial phenomenon could be. We have not developed any theoretical models for this network yet, as we developed theoretical, if not always very useful, models for the old. (Try applying central place theory to our new landscape.) Such models will be vastly different, more complex, and less spatial than those for the old. One of the differences between the systems is that of recognizable order. Older agricultural landscapes inevitably have a clear visual order, built from visual patterns, building materials of local origin (or a national order, in the case of the railroad and the balloon frame), and a settlement system of residences, service, and market towns, and transport routes. It is that order, and the contrapuntal variety within it, that leads us to describe landscapes like the Cotswolds as a Platonic essence made visible.

As to the new rural landscape, I offer three observations. First, it does not, cannot, and should not partake of any older rural order. Second, we do not yet know and cannot envision what this new landscape's ultimate order might be. Third, this new landscape, because it is so far less deterministic than an agricultural landscape, is likely to have an apparent (conventionally recognizable?) order only by design, whether or not that design comes from designers.

The new and the old landscapes are two inherently different networks that somehow have to coexist or find resolution on the same land. This concept is different not only from the metaphor of nasty residential development seeping out like a virus from the city and interstates but also from Lewis's old city and new city. The galactic metropolis that Lewis sees surrounds, engulfs, and eventually transforms the old city. The new and the old rural landscape grids have no such clear, clean, and easy deterministic relation. Exploring the relation between them would be the next task after understanding more about the new network itself.

Where does this leave us in terms of understanding what this new composite landscape might look like? The first task, that of understanding the new landscape network on its own terms, suggests two needs. First we need a new vocabulary. I have said that old categories such as town, village, hamlet, and farmstead are no longer relevant. For example, what terms should the census bureau use to characterize this new landscape? I'm not knowledgeable enough to comment definitively, but it seems that "nonrural farm" is much too coarse grained a category to make much sense of what's going on.

The second need is to analyze—not only conceptualizing but also describing and quantifying, observing and documenting—what is going on. Countless questions pop up. Are there regional differences? Are patterns of the new landscape different in different parts of the country because of differences in prosperity? Does prosperity, in fact, spur physical expression of the new landscape? What are the demographics of the people who are building this new landscape grid on the land—are they young or old, retired or employed, rich or poor? Do land uses in various agricultural regions of the United States make a major difference in the physical expressions of the new landscape on the land? What difference do local tax structures and landholding practices make?

As a designer thinking about the form of this new landscape, I first wonder what people seek there. What motivates people who move to the countryside, not to work on it, but solely to live on it and thereby create a new landscape? We might frame some general questions to ask them.

Some of the questions would explore reasons that have nothing to do with what we think of as landscape issues. There are all sorts of reasons that people might have for moving to the countryside which have little to do with the affective impact of a rural landscape as we understand it and study it. Easy travel, cheap land, permissive building codes (or none at all), tax structures, the absence of minorities in schools—all of these might be important considerations of only indirect connection to the landscape experience. They are important, but they are locational issues, in contrast to landscape issues.

Obviously, another set of questions deals with whether and why people move to the countryside in search of a particular landscape experience.

Overlaying new nonagricultural phenomena (such as houses) onto the old grid seems to be producing three conceptually different patterns. I will call them Eden I, II, and III.

In Eden I, the new house sits in the existing or old rural framework without really affecting it. An isolated house makes little visual impact on the existing landscape; when one is in the house or next to it, all one sees is the traditional rural landscape. At the other extreme, Eden III establishes a scale and pattern sufficient to create a completely new environment within itself. In the Illinois flatlands, Eden III is typically an amenity subdivision clustered along a stream corridor, in stark contrast with the surrounding landscape. These subdivisions are treed and curvilinear, versus the open and rectilinear surrounding landscape.

Eden II, common here in central Illinois, is particularly interesting and, I think, alarming. I call it "septic-tank strip suburbia." It commonly results when a farmer sells land fronting the road along one side of a farm, subdivided into small urban-sized parcels. One way to characterize this Eden is as ingeniously combining the worst of town and country living with the advantages of neither. A perhaps less pejorative characterization is that it vitiates the landscape experience of the existing or traditional land pattern without being strong or extensive enough to substitute a pattern or environment of its own.

These conceptual qualities suggest some of the questions that we might ask new rural residents. What were the important factors in their decision to move to the countryside? What environmental amenities were they seeking? What about the new landscape, and the older, which often surrounds it, do they most like or dislike? What would make the new landscape more livable or enjoyable for them? Do these newcomers think of themselves as living in the "country"?

The point of these questions is to learn something about what kind of landscape, if any, these new rural residents might be seeking. Do they have a vision of landscape? If the newcomers do have a landscape vision, it might not be one that we appreciate or even understand. Their vision of the countryside might be very different from ours as designers, planners, or public officials. If so, we should know it.

On the other hand, if we understand what these people are looking for, it might enable us to find design forms for it and to turn our attention not to minimizing the presence of the new landscape in the countryside but to expressing it as itself, for itself, in some sort of landscape vision.

Understanding a vision for the new landscape, we might be able to go beyond trying to preserve the character of the old, to envision ways in which both the old and the new landscape can have physical expressions that do not destroy one another but coexist with, or even complement, one another. Is it naive to think that as designers and planners of the rural landscape we could develop such a vision? I do not think so. Whatever we think of suburbia, there was in the nineteenth century a moving and powerful vision among designers of what suburbia might and should be. Whatever we think of the emptiness of the City Beautiful, it also had a powerful visual and physical image.

If the idea of the new rural landscape is as powerful, as different, as important as I think it is, it deserves such an image and it would be worthwhile to work on it. Surely our countryside deserves more than hiding a new landscape, confining it to nonproductive farmland, or giving it curved streets with names from Walter Scott novels in whatever ¼-¼-¼ section a farmer is willing to sell. Is it naive to think that such an image might make a real difference in the shape and working of our countryside? Maybe. But that does not mean it is not worth trying.

How do we begin? First by using our eyes to see what is out there, what exactly sits on the land and where. Edge City might now be a more illuminating phrase than urban sprawl, but it remains an easy categorization that short-circuits observation and reflection.

Second, we need to consider why what is there is there. This requires a deep sense of local and regional history, a knowledge of the landscape as a complex, evolving artifact, a particular and peculiar place expression of larger social and cultural trends. Regional landscapes are understandable only as combinations of the local and the global, the genus loci and the Zeitgeist. Regional and local history is out of fashion, conjuring up images of cardigan-clad antiquarians, or naive New Deal populists. But intelligent planning requires this history. Who teaches this? Must each of us learn it on our own?

Third, because the new rural landscape is created largely by new people moving into the countryside, we must understand what they seek, their ideal landscape. When we add knowledge of the constraints, both regional and cultural, within which both choice and design must operate, maybe, as designers and planners, we might be prepared to assemble a new vision for that landscape.

⚜ ⚜ ⚜ ⚜ The Indeterminate Eye: Place and People in Three Decades of Landscape Photography

> But the nearest I have ever come to
> fishing on the Susquehanna
> was one afternoon in a museum in Philadelphia
>
> when I balanced a little egg of time
> in front of a painting
> in which that river curled around a bend
>
> under a blue cloud-ruffled sky,
> dense trees along the banks,
> and a fellow with a red bandanna
>
> sitting in a small, green
> flat-bottom boat
> holding the thin whip of a pole.
>
> —Billy Collins, "Fishing on the Susquehanna in July"

Landscape photography is built upon a series of transactions between an object/subject, an interpreter, an image, and another interpreter. The landscape is object and subject, the image a two-dimensional photograph, and the interpreters are artist and reader, respectively. I use "reader" not to imply the fashionable designation of any environmental phenomenon or experience as "text," but because it is appropriate: as more active than the term "viewer" and less pejorative than "consumer." In calling the landscape at least partially an object, I am flouting at least a quarter century's rejection of the idea of object and objectivity, rejection of nature as "out there" for the idea of nature as a cultural construct, and the common lament of designers-would-be-philosophers that the "objectification of our landscape" is the root cause of our twenty-first-century malaise. The landscape is an object. So, too, landscape is a subject and our relationships with it partly subjective. Even a naive and untutored viewer (that term is appropriate here) can match a landscape with its photograph with more or less ease, proof that at least some degree of objectivity exists in the process. Objectivity comes in degrees, just as subjectivity does. All photographs are both objective and subjective, to a greater or lesser degree, a degree contingent upon the receptive stance of the reader and other transactions.

The indeterminacy in variability of objective/subjective in the interpretation of landscape by an artist parallels a similar indeterminacy in the relation between the artist's interpretation, the reader's interpretation of that take, and the interpretations of different readers. This can be blatant when a narrative element dominates the image . . . a point I learned from my own teaching. Richard Bergh's 1900 painting *Nordic Summer Evening* is from a school and period of Nordic landscape painting often characterized as reassuring the bourgeoisie through the appropriation of nature as property, or some such. Specifically, the critic Kirk Varnedoe saw here unease and tension between the man and woman because the sensuality of the mellow late-night landscape was raising sexual thoughts in each of them. My graduate students, when asked to supply a narrative for the painting, identify the same themes but reverse the causality, the majority reading the situation as that of two people, uncomfortable and tense with the sexual communication between them, coping by averting their gaze from one another and staring out into the landscape for distraction and dissembling. This "objective" consensus at one level supporting subjective interpretation at another is probably typical of most landscape image reading.

Some current landscape scholars advance serious landscape photography as valuable documentation of our ordinary landscape. Others leap from the artist's choice of focal length and camera angle to the conclusion that landscape photographs are always primarily subjective interpretations based on social and artistic biases. In fact, the truth and validity of these assertions lie in the reader as well as the artist in any particular case. We must move beyond the mantra of the subjectivity of photography (a concern a century and a half old, as Martin Jay has pointed out) to understand the role and range of landscape photography as experience. That experience combines objectivity and subjectivity, giving landscape photography its potential for art experience and, as well, abuse.

This essay concentrates on the relationship between reader, landscape, and landscape experience. I will offer little or nothing about the formal parameters (e.g., composition, tonality, artistic genealogy) and little about "social construction of vision," either in terms of the role of the visual image in our society in general or its manipulation by agencies and powers within that society. I deal with neither connoisseurship nor context, but with experience.

But it is important first to consider one aspect of the social and cultural context of experiencing landscape images. The contrast of landscape photography with landscape painting illuminates several aspects of this relationship. Landscape painting is a genre as old as the Renaissance. Landscape photography has existed for less than a century and a half and accepted as an art form for even less. Landscape paintings make up a significant part of most museum's collections (in the case of mountain or seaside resort village museums, probably the major part), while photographs, usually displayed in commercial galleries devoted solely to that purpose, when they reach the level of museum exhibitions, are often relegated to banal basement spaces less carefully staged than those galleries for medieval Japanese armor, and appear in a less "museum-like" context. Paintings are mounted in frames of varying degrees of elaboration, photographs mounted simply with a white margin and minimal frames. Most landscape images, like most paintings, are experienced not on walls but in books, where the photographic reproductions usually approximate the size and format of their hung originals more than do reproductions of paintings.

These differences can be interpreted variously, but they clearly confirm the socially superior cachet of painting among the traditional guardians of the arts. I submit two additional characterizations. First, because fewer immediate and apparent filters, or layers of abstraction and presentation, operate when viewing a photograph compared to a painting, the reader is more likely to search for a "real" landscape in photographs. Similarly the reader finds fewer impediments in appropriating the photographic image into his or her internal psychic landscape experience. The leap that Billy Collins, with a poet's sensitivity, made from Herman Herzog's painting *Fishing on the Susquehanna* to his own experience seems more typical in a reading of a landscape photograph than in a painting. Facing a landscape photograph, the reader will likely not only posit a real landscape but more likely process it into his or her internal landscape. The photograph's power to do this lies in its dual role of surrogate and stimulus.

No landscape image is the truth; all landscape images offer partial truths. All landscape images are more or less valuable as experiential resonances or, in Gary Winogrand's phrase, "figments." The oscillating referral between landscape and landscape image is a continuous psychic process in which each influences the other in shifting ways over time. Our understanding of the landscape out there grows richer and more complex with each landscape truth we learn. So our internal psychic landscape, that important and powerful landscape in shaping our life experiences, grows ever richer and more complex as we accumulate fragments of landscape experience, both imaginary and real.

If these claims correspond to our experience, then it is worthwhile asking what changes have happened to landscape and landscape image, as both surrogate and stimulus, over three decades of rapid and radical changes in landscape photography.

Some of these changes simply parallel, and document, changes in the landscape that are in fact "out there." Others might reasonably be predicted from a general familiarity with postmodern postures and vocabularies. Others, however, are less predictable, more provocative, and raise questions about the landscape experience itself.

Without too much oversimplification we can divide the history of landscape photography in America into four stages. The first began with the early railroad surveys of the American West and later the work of Carleton Watkins and others, glorifying human intervention and the reconstructing of that landscape. These photographs served as documents and as a psychosocial justification for exploitation but also corrected the romantic west of Albert Bierstadt and others who brought the Hudson River into the arid West, where there were no misty vistas in soft light, but raw, barren, aggressively barren, landscapes. As the frontier and its mentality passed, a later school of photography saw landscape as a source of purity and beauty, a transcendental landscape expressed in the careful modeling of light and shadow, and the dominant figure of Ansel Adams, whose presence and sense of publicity dominated, to some extent oppressed, decades of landscape photographers. In the third phase photographers began to imbue nature and the landscape with social and political significance. The roots of this movement overlap the school of transcendental beauty, in the 1930s and '40s, when Walker Evans, Dorothea Lange, and others worked at the same time as the transcendentalists. A fourth stage, around and enveloping us now, is not characterized so easily but surely qualifies for the all-purpose adjective of postmodern. Symptomatic of that phrase in our times, it shows many divergent landscapes and approaches, some of which we will examine.

The 1970s are a good starting point to reflect upon the vast number of changes since Ansel Adams. In 1963 the Sierra Club published *The Place No One Knew*, Eliot Porter's monumental work in Glen Canyon, documenting a landscape soon to be submerged by waters backed up by a dam. His semiabstract images of the rocks and plants and waters of the canyon in gorgeous, saturated colors became the apogee and bible of color nature photography. But then in 1972 the Sierra Club published a far less known work, *Floor of the Sky*, photographs of the Great Plains by David Plowden. For the first time a Sierra Club book included human artifacts and utilitarian, everyday landscapes. This was also the heyday of the photorealist painters, when Richard Estes, Ralph Goings, and others violated traditional boundaries between painting and photography. In doing so, they often glamorized, if sometimes with a subtext of irony, the same ordinary human landscape that Plowden and others were photographing.

The later 1970s also witnessed three remarkable, if less known, *rephotographic* works. Thomas Vale and Georgina Vale followed George Stewart's monumental 1950 journey along U.S. 40, taking photographs from the same spots as Stewart had. In *Second View*, several photographers combined to rephotograph selected images from nineteenth-century railway surveys, and Bill Ganzel in *Dust Bowl Descent* revisited the sites, even some of the people, from the Farm Security Administration photographs of forty years before. Even casual readers of these photographs lost any simplistic message or interpretation of American landscape change. In many cases, particularly in the rephotographing of the railway surveys, what seemed disruption and ugliness in the early photographs had become nearly pastoralized with the passage of time. Other landscapes, Vale and Vale noted, had changed hardly at all. Landscape change was uneven and unpredictable. Frank Gohlke's photographs of grain elevators in the same decade epitomize the photographers' new landscape lens. From the 1920s through the 1940s the great grain terminals of ports and cities had been romanticized as emblems of American power in Charles Sheeler's paintings and Walker Evans's photographs. By the 1950s Wright Morris was finding in small country elevators a simple direct beauty, using prose as well as photos to characterize them as products of their makers and their dwellers. He saw nostalgic, melancholy reminders of the passage of time and changes in our landscape and society. But now others began to see the elevator in a different role, not as a symbol of industrial might, not as a nostalgic remnant, but as buildings embedded in the towns and the society and the economic system they supported. These elevators are not romanticized nor are they admirable architectural objects. They visually and socially dominate the towns they stand in as they did in real life, with little hint of charm or abstract beauty.

The most dramatic impact of the new landscape photography came in 1975, when the International Museum of Photography at George Eastman House assembled the exhibit *New Topographics: Photographs of a Man-Altered Landscape*. The exhibit and the ensuing catalog probably did more to change landscape photography in this country than any other single event or publication. The landscape of these photographers was not beautiful, or ordered, or productive. They captured a new American landscape of disorder, arbitrariness, ennui, and anomie. Their images of trailer parks and raw western suburbs were to become icons as powerful as those of Ansel Adams decades earlier, and echoes of their work remain in many contemporary photographic exhibits.

In this new landscape photography there are few or no heroes, no John Muirs or John Waynes. The explorers and the trappers are gone, replaced by sunbathers in Yosemite and tourists photographing from the top of

Glen Canyon dam. Nature, long a stable source of romanticization, is now problematic. Kudzu fills southern landscape photographs with ambivalence, a foreground of both decay and regeneration, as an invasive and destructive plant nostalgically shrouds architectural remains. Photographers traveled to the national parks not for pristine transcendental beauty but for photographs of campers and recreational vehicles, a landscape less of beauty than of a new bourgeois leisure, Monument Valley seen framed by an open car door. Ambivalence pervades these photographs. Robert Adams in *Summer Nights* produced some of the most succinct and beautiful vistas of small-town America ever captured, during the same years when he was photographing a Los Angeles landscape whose images sighed of emptiness and of neglect or at least of disregard.

If Robert Adams's ambivalence was pensive, reflective, and maybe a bit mournful, by the '90s the sigh of ambivalence had become a strident scream. Conflict between nature and technology becomes a dominant theme; deplorable scenes of destruction combine with vivid, beautiful renderings of almost unearthly color: nature taking over the bunkers of Pacific atoll nuclear tests, images of fire-gutted black and yellow school buses in the atomic wastes of the Nevada desert, and pipelines through vividly polluted southern swamps, Three Mile Island, color-saturated industrial fumes, and visions of Technicolor technological circuses in hell. Lucy Lippard called this a time of "revisionists contradicting cherished landscape fantasies, juggling terrifying messages with the inherent beauty of the landscape, the unexpectedly gorgeous pollution generated colors, and compelling textures of blasted and flagellated surfaces." Maybe these photographers directly express a larger cultural ambivalence. Maybe they simply cannot escape the seductive beckoning of saturated hues and richly textured surfaces. More likely, both.

A few photographers of the last three decades reached a less judgmental acceptance of the ordinary landscape, neither the romanticism of Adams and Weston's New Mexico villages nor the polemic of alienation and anomie of the New Topographics' Front Range trailer camps. Alex Harris photographed the Hispanic uplands of New Mexico as a symbiosis between landscape, towns and cars, and a place-specific culture which, strangely, recalls on the one hand the early photographs of Paul Strand and on the other Bernice Abbott's New York work in the '30s and the Farm

Security Administration figures of that decade. Not surprisingly, much current work has to do with the road and the American propensity for movement and travel, with a flood of coffee table books on U.S. 66 and other now-sanctified relics, as one generation's blight becomes another generation's nostalgic kitsch. But more important are the photographs of streets, roads, parking lots, motels, and airports evolving from Gary Winogrand's work. Geoff Winningham has captured the ironies, the drabness, and the ordinariness of Houston streets, and the nature, the roads and streets, and the parking structures of Chicago suburbia. Jose Camilo Vergara shows us rats, abandoned shopping carts, rotting sofas, and dog carcasses, but also the almost neutral remnants of the 1970 riots, such as an empty, almost pastoral avenue in Detroit and the rebuilding along freeways in once devastated urban renewal areas. All these views of the American landscape are the more provocative for their complexity and ambiguity.

This new respect for the ordinary landscape, falling somewhere between resignation and the fondness of familiarity, comes across at its most vivid in the work of Joel Sternfeld and Stephen Shore. Shore's stance has been described as one of "stubborn neutrality," perhaps a parallel to the writings of J. B. Jackson, the detached and semidistant outsider looking for the insider's view, interpreting it, capturing it, the old-fashioned anthropologist become photographer. Their work epitomizes the blend, in this case the balance, of objectivity and subjectivity that is the core of powerful landscape photography.

Above all, the landscape photography of the last three decades has loosened and deeply problematized the relation between people and the landscape in which they live or through which they move. Older landscape photographs showed peoples as inhabitants of their landscape, whether Native Americans, or miners of the Old West, or Paul Strand's villagers. They portrayed and assumed a stable long-term relationship, a bonding between person and land. Early blows to this assumed bond reach back to at least mid-century in the works of Gary Winogrand, traveling throughout the United States, and in Robert Frank's seminal *The Americans,* where we first find a distanced relation of uncertainty, of change, of flux, always in doubt. Often it rests on a sense of alienation, as in Frank's classic picture of a men's room shoeshine described by Jack Kerouac as "the loneliest picture ever made, the urinals that women never see, the shoe-shine going on in sad eternity." Its nuances today are persuasively captured by Joel Sternfeld in his book *Stranger Passing: Woman with Mail, Golfer Teeing Off, Woman Changing Attire for a Business Meeting, Lawyer with Laundry,* spectacularly in the *Web Site Designer Walking Home,* and surely the *A Young Man Gathering Shopping Carts,* a picture my students retitled *Parking Lot Adonis.* These landscapes could be anywhere. Photographers have given up trying to capture some Platonic essence of place. It is not that these people have no relationship at all with the pictured landscape, but that the relationship is a transient one of change and flux, beyond the reader's capacity to determine, a complexity of variability and unpredictability. These are the landscapes of apartness.

But while human bonds to the landscape wither, some photographers in the first decade of a new century hint at a new landscape sensitivity, of an entirely new concept of landscape, or more appropriately, of the landscape experience.

The chimerical relationship between person and land, between the encounter and the experience, between the seen and the felt, between the out there and the landscape of the mind, is parallel to a new way of conceiving the landscape experience. Old traditions and simple assumptions about that relationship have disappeared in a web of complex questions and interactions. Environmental determinism had its sway, remarkably, until a very few decades ago, long past the French geographers of the early twentieth century, and still finds echoes in the travel writing of Lawrence Durrell and others. The English Augustans categorized archetypical landscapes and tied them to certain sensibilities. They spoke only to their own elite, incestuous circles, but they considered the principles universal and reachable by people of education and enlightenment. Ruskin added melodramatic overtones in a mix of grandeur and weather, and Hamerton, Ruskin's follower, even associated personality types with certain landscapes, whether by nature or nurture. As recently as two decades ago, we believed wholeheartedly in visual assessment, which assumed that preferences were stable and could be determined, and implicitly assumed that the primary relationship to the landscape was visual, static, and scenic. People varied only as molecules in Brownian motion, and the overall picture could be captured in statistics, a belief carried to caricature in the landscape paintings of Komar and Melamid. We believed in determinacy, analysis, and categorization.

Some forty years ago David Lowenthal wrote "The American Scene," a work I taught from for many years. Now we ask *whose* American scene? For Lowenthal it was an American landscape and image created and sanctified in the respectable writing of travelers, essayists, and the media. Today we look at that landscape through a number of different lenses: age, race, gender, class, and ethnicity. In the last two decades, we have come to realize that much of our relationship to the landscape, and indeed the bulk of some people's experiences, is built from those transient, traveling existences portrayed so vividly in John Updike's short story "The City." It can be built from displacement and ambiguity among Native Americans in landscape, as sketched by N. Scott Momaday, Louise Erdrich, and Sherman Alexie; from immigrants in the work of Maxine Hong Kingston and Bharati Mukherjee; and on to the cosmopolitan, reflective wanderings of V. S. Naipaul, Edward Said, and André Aciman. We now deal with landscapes of expatriation and repatriation, of exile, of poverty and urban migration, and massive displacement. The once normative landscape of stability and bonding has been problematized almost out of existence. The overpowering contemporary message is of people apart from a landscape, not as citizens of their landscape. Heideggerian indwelling and Teutonic *Heimat* are now but memories.

Our experience of the landscape depends on what we bring to it. Whether beyond or within the constraints and strictures of culture, colonialism, capitalism, and class, all so dear to our academic revisionism, we experience the landscape as individuals. We bring memories, not just as a scrapbook but as an old trunk in our attic, filled with the jumble of mental and psychic bits and pieces from a past. We bring a kaleidoscope of thousands of film and magazine images from our media-saturated past and present. We bring our present, a loose gestalt of expectations, mood, physical condition, and mental state. As Aciman has noted, we can even bring anticipation of landscapes to come.

The more interesting of today's landscape photography comes to grips with this interior/exterior landscape of experience, a landscape not only of apartness but of indeterminacy. Digital manipulation allows the artist to remove, insert, condense, combine, distort, join, merge, but still offer that photographic guarantee of a "real" landscape. This work is different and distinct from the dark-room manipulation of a couple of decades ago: those photographs portraying marble columns and entablatures resting on water, or doorways showing an entrance from a known world to some fantasy landscape. In those earlier works the manipulation was as blatant as the symbolism, with its references to Jungian archetypes and reminders of the surreal landscapes of De Chirico and Dali. In newer work we sense not permanence but recent formation and imminent disappearance. These landscapes, on first sight, sometimes even after concentrated study, just might be "real" landscapes, or typical landscape experiences. Steps lead down from a New Mexico mesa onto the turf of Central Park, two businessmen among a crowded street are blazingly illuminated, even as they are isolated in crowded noncommunication, a hyena snarls from the undergrowth in Rock Creek Park, a sign of Vegas glitz arises from a stoop-labor field, or an entirely imaginary, fantastic, but yet understandable landscape is composed.

Pedro Meyer's work is probably the most forceful and explicit of these new landscape manipulations and constructions. His book is as ambiguous as his photographs, juxtaposing "original" and "manipulated" images identifiable as one or the other only by the date given in small caption type. Very different are the fantasies of Sally Mann (yes, that Sally Mann), the most magical and convincing evocations of "garden" that I have ever seen.

These photo manipulations, however "legitimate" or not as "photography," capture rich interior landscapes that might, or might not, lurk behind that indeterminate relationship of strangers crossing parking lots. Photographers as different as Meyers from Sternfeld, or Shore from Mann, affirm the landscape of apartness and indeterminacy; the landscape of many truths and many fragments affirms that, for better or worse, place is increasingly built on displacements, shards, and unlikely linkages.

Note

This essay was written with the help of Rachel Leibowitz, a skilled guide through the world of contemporary landscape images. She should not, however, be held responsible for all of the speculations advanced here.

◢ ◢ ◢ ◢ Authority and Insecurity

Looking back after six decades spent in the design academy I remember, uncomfortably, being bombarded with a succession of intellectual hero figures from other disciplines, the rhetorical hooks on which to hang our design decisions. There were Darcy Thompson on growth and form, C. West Churchman on systems, Herbert Simon on administrative behavior, Ludwig von Bertalanffy on general systems theory, W. R. Ashby on cybernetics and homeostasis, Jean Piaget on childhood development, Claude Lévi-Strauss on bricolage and dualities, Italo Calvino, Umberto Eco, Gilles Deleuze and his rhizomes, and so on, an architectural propensity first noted over fifty years ago by John Summerson in "The Mischievous Analogy." Landscape architecture has not been innocent of such fads and frivolities, but they have usually been on a less pretentious intellectual level, more derived from reading *Newsweek* than the *New York Review of Books*—left brain/right brain, future shock, fractals—but still I regret our lost innocence every time I encounter the supposed sophistication assumed to come with using words like praxis, chronos, or topos in today's writings.

All of the phenomena and the authors above have had valuable insights toward a better understanding of design and the environment. But they have been used as rhetorical justifications and badges of intellectual sophistication, not applied in the real process of design and understanding (even assuming that were possible). When they have later been discarded to make room for newer fashions, no intellectual tools or underpinnings have remained for our use. If we were to turn to any of these authors and those concepts today we would have to start all over. That is not intellectual progress, it is harlotry.

Grappling with new ideas is intense and exciting. Using the rhetoric and not the idea throws away the chance to bring serious thought into a parochial discipline.

❀ ❀ ❀ ❀ Some Thoughts on Scholarship and Publication

I have within the last year participated in four conference sessions discussing the current state of scholarship and graduate education in environmental design.[1] The major concern of the educators at these meetings can be expressed simply: raising the standards of scholarship and research, while maintaining both a diversity of approaches and some sense of relevance to real-world design—the bettering of the human environment. What follow are fragments and pieces of my own concern.

On Scholarship and Research

Research is a magic word. Its effects on the design disciplines have been mixed. On the one hand, there is a pride in our doing research, a pride that we are part of the scientific and intellectual community. On the other hand, there is a sloppiness about the use of the word that produces confusion about what we are doing and why. The term research is used far too broadly. At one extreme, we recognize a narrow model of research from the experimental or laboratory sciences: the posing of a hypothesis, the designing of a method to test the hypothesis, the testing itself, conclusions, modification of the hypothesis, and so on. At the other extreme, our undergraduate students, flipping through magazines the first week of a design project, are "doing their library research." Somewhere in this fascination with the magic aura of research, the idea of scholarship has gotten lost.

Is this just a semantic quibble? Beyond the vague feeling that research and scholarship are not identical modes of inquiry, is anything to be gained by examining how the two words are used? The recent social etymology of the words is certainly distinct. Not only does research have connotations of the laboratory and experiments, it has a mystique that has pervaded American society and universities since the Manhattan Project. Research is glamorous. Research produces bigger bombs, faster Fords, and cancer cures. Scholarship produces intellectual masturbation on the use of verb forms in Chaucer. Real folk do research, wearing hard hats or laboratory smocks. Quiche folk do scholarship, wearing cardigans and corduroys.

Research has even become a verb (though not here, thank you). Can we imagine a verb "to scholar"? Imagine the American Society of Landscape Architects Annual Awards Program including scholarship awards as well as research awards? Imagine referring to our institutions as major scholarship universities? Not likely. Does it matter? Yes, it does. First, precision in the use of words is never amiss. Second, the rush to use the word research to cover almost anything that isn't teaching or service leads to sloppy thinking and sloppy standards.

Finally, the implicit tendency to model ourselves on quantitative, or laboratory, or experimental, or whatever, sciences has even affected the format of what we write, and thereby how we think. Two small examples are the use of citations and abstracts. In the experimental sciences, citations are commonly used to base work upon earlier experiments in the same line. In these fields, one commonly assumes that the findings referred to have been "proven." In the speculative, humanist tradition, this is very different. A reference to Jay Appleton, for example, does not prove that human beings react to the environment in terms of prospect and refuge; it only establishes that Appleton suggests they do. And yet as the editor of a journal I constantly get manuscripts from authors who don't know the difference. This is the phenomenon I call "authority by repetitive citation." It is a good example of low standards of thought in our discipline.

Similarly, the role of abstracts is different in laboratory sciences and in a field such as ours. In most established hard sciences, an abstract can give a fair idea of both the meaning and the quality of a paper, assuming the author is neither negligent nor fabricating. This is because the fields are narrowly focused and paradigms are well defined and universally accepted. In a field such as ours, an abstract conveys no idea of the quality of the paper and often little even of the content. One of the marks of our maturity as a discipline will be when conference organizers insist on reviewing complete manuscripts and not abstracts.

On Professions and Disciplines

Academic landscape architecture is in transition from a profession to a discipline. The concerns and the activities of our academic world are no longer driven by the world of practice and applications. For years, academics in the applied and fine arts have been accepted as members of the academic community without being expected to conform to its standards. Environmental designers within the academy did essentially the same things, or addressed the same issues, as those in the outside world. Practitioners faulted the schools for how well or poorly they prepared students for practice, but there was never any question that that was what the universities were doing, however well or badly.

That time is passing, maybe past. Academic landscape architects are doing things that are not done in professional practice. Some of these, like environment-behavior studies, are unique to academia because the world of practice has yet to realize their utility, or because the state of knowledge has not advanced to the point that such studies are usable in actual design. Other activities going on in the universities, like the scholarly study of landscape architecture itself, will probably never be done in practice. This is only an aspect of the change, however.

Landscape architectural educators are becoming less like their practitioner cousins, more like their academic colleagues. The academic design world is becoming a subculture of its own, distinct from the world of practice. The growth of this separation, which the classic modern movement fought to avoid, is a subject for study in itself as an exercise in the sociology of disciplines. But it is certainly clear that the academic design community now communicates largely with itself, has established its own set of awards and peer recognition, socializes its children, provides rites of passage, and above all poses its own questions and develops its own paradigms distinct from, and sometimes irrelevant to, the world of practice.

This is as much a cause of the lack of communication between the practitioners and academics as it is a result. It is not conformity forced on us by academic administrators. Our constraints come less from administrators than from ourselves and our peers and are reinforced by promotion and tenure hysteria. Not only are the questions we seek to answer often distinct from those in practice, but they will undergo cycles of fashion all their own, equally remote from, and irrelevant to, practice. There is a cycle of fashion in academic preoccupations as much as in design styles. Whether we view all this as maturation or degeneration, as problem or opportunity, it seems inevitable.

Other fields have been there before us. Different fields have developed different relationships between study and application, between discipline and profession. The form of the distinction in medicine is not the same as in law, and neither is the same as that in music. Such speculation can be amusing but also frightening. Could environmental design be headed to an eventual split as radical as that between English and journalism in our universities?

On Magazines and Journals

If these traits distinguish between two sociological subcultures, the issues are not so clear intellectually or ideologically. There are a number of people out there, subculture or not, who think they are doing something akin to design "scholarship." I suppose they think of themselves as design theoreticians. They are a mix, ranging from art and architectural historians to academic teachers of design theory to high-style practitioners who appear in full color on the cover of *Metropolis* or *Landscape Architecture* magazine and issue theoretical pronouncements. Often these folks have a loose, half-time, adjunct relationship to the academy. Much of the visual, spatial, and even intellectual excitement in the design world comes from them. But can we classify them as academics or practitioners only? Consider publications. We all know that practitioners have magazines and scholars have journals. On this basis, it's easy to distinguish between, say, the old *Progressive Architecture* on the one hand and the *Journal of Architecture Planning Research* on the other, between *Landscape Architecture* magazine and *Landscape Journal*. But there are influential periodicals that do not easily fit into this dichotomy of professional, ad-filled magazines versus scholarly journals. How about, for example, *Space and Society, Oppositions, Places,* or *Landscape*?[2] They commonly publish provocative and speculative musings of an orientation and quality that seldom show up in the conventional magazines or conventional journals. It is an exercise in these distinctions, or lack of distinctions, to think how you might decide between sending an article to *Landscape Journal* or to *Landscape* or *Places*. This is important not only because we live in a media-dominated society where so much of our intellectual communication takes place in print but also because much of our best philosophy, criticism, and speculation comes from these "in between" publications.

On Theory and Pseudotheory

"Theory" probably shares with "sense of place" the award for our most misused term of recent decades. There are two important differences in the use of these two terms, however. First, sense of place will no doubt pass out of fashion before too long.[3] The word theory has been around a long time and probably always will be around. The other difference is that sense of place is a real-world phenomenon, of acknowledged importance if difficult definition, and is, of necessity, a fuzzy set. Theory, however, is a concept and a definition and can be as discrete and unequivocal as we wish it to be. Unfortunately, the definition of theory as landscape architects use it is simple. Anything concerned with *what* to do or *why* to do it, instead of *how* to do it, is proudly proclaimed as theory. This is not theory; this is pseudotheory. In addition to this broad and sloppy definition, pseudotheory is characterized by two other properties.

Pseudotheory Is Plagiarized from Other Disciplines

Such justificatory borrowing goes back at least as far as Palladio, but has been a dominant theme of architecture from Viollet-le-Duc through modernism to postmodernism. John Summerson put it well four decades ago: "The Modern Architect . . . has, for some reason or another, stepped out of his role, taken a look at the scene around him and then become obsessed with the importance not of architecture, but of the relation of architecture to other things."

Thus we have had banal biomorphism (aka the word "organic"), pseudosemiology, and now decorative deconstructionism. We also currently have flatulo-phenomenology; but to give it justice, phenomenology as a philosophy or an epistemology, not a theory, and as used by Europeans, not North Americans, has made serious contributions. Readers interested in thinking about this topic should read Summerson or Peter Collins. I will mention only briefly my discomfort with one currently most fashionable mode of pseudotheory. Deconstructionism is a mode of literary analysis. The simplistic inference made by our high-style design pundits—that a complex of theory and methods designed to investigate a literary text is equally valid for the built environment—is an example of the superficiality and lack of disciplined thought that pervades the design world. In fact, serious discussion about ways in which buildings and landscapes are similar to literature in the perceptions of their consumers and ways in which they aren't would be thought provoking. The mind-jerk assumption of their equivalence is but nonsense. It typifies our inability, or unwillingness, to distinguish model from metaphor, analysis from analogy, and theory from framework.

Pseudotheory Follows Form and Seeks to Justify It

Styles can be thought of as having their own life cycles, susceptible to study apart from the society in which they are embedded. Many historians of art have taken this approach. Proponents of a new design style, however, particularly in situations where its acceptance depends on publicity, justify it in terms of larger social or intellectual profundities. An extreme example of this was heard at a recent Associated Collegiate Schools of Architecture meeting. The familiar postmodern was justified on the basis of what we have "learned" from science, more specifically, physics. Einstein's theory of relativity and Heisenberg's uncertainty principle were used both to justify the particular design solution and to discredit classic modernism as a valid aesthetic vocabulary for our time, Einstein and Heisenberg having proven the futility of a unitary interpretation. The irony, unmentioned at the conference, is that the sixty-year-old bible of classic modernism, Giedion's *Space, Time, and Architecture,* used exactly the same argument to justify the modernist architectural revolution and discredit the Beaux-Arts eclecticism that preceded it. We should be able to laugh at this, but so many design schools take such silliness so seriously that laughter rings hollow.

On Theories, Models, and Frameworks

A plea for more restrictive and more precise use of the word theory is not in conflict with the plea for diversity of methods and approaches. Precision, per se, is seldom out of place. Further, by making clear what we are doing and not doing, restricted use of the term theory should, in fact, support a diversity of approaches, a point to which I shall return.

The definitions that I find most useful in this arena are those of Amos Rapoport, who distinguishes between frameworks, models, and theories. Put in simplest terms, a theory explains, a model predicts, and a framework organizes. A framework can be judged on its reasonableness and its utility, but claims no exclusivity vis-à-vis other frameworks. If we accept these definitions, it is clear that most theories or philosophies of design are not theories at all, but frameworks. Philosophies of design are intellectual and verbal frameworks that organize ideas, just as styles can be thought of as visual frameworks that organize tangible things. Design theory or philosophy, then, is often a sociocultural framework serving as a justification for a visual framework.

Aphorisms form a fourth, and useful, intellectual category. Maybe the design world has used aphorisms more than other fields, but that is another topic. What is clear is that expressions such as "form follows function," or "architecture is frozen music," or "less is more" are merchandising slogans for visual frameworks or styles.

This takes us back to the second advantage of using a restrictive definition of theory. By distinguishing among the four classes of aphorisms, frameworks, models, and theories, we clearly see what stage of intellectual certainty or utility we have established with any given statement. But there is also a curious fringe benefit. Some famous aphorisms, maxims of design, are in fact translatable to theories capable of being tested. Of the three examples quoted above, one—"less is more"—falls most obviously into this category. We can paraphrase Mies's maxim as "economy in formal expression produces greater affective impact upon the beholder." (That there are other equally reasonable translations points to a critical difference between an aphorism and a theory, and partly explains the persuasive power of the former.) A social scientist could test this generality in specific, controlled experiments. Maybe the relationship between aphorisms and theories can be seen as another expression of the relationship between the "aesthetic" and the "behavioral" approaches to design—the critical design schism of our time.

Surely it is clear that the first step in building a valid, useful theory of design must be understanding what a theory is. The second step is to realize that, while aphorisms might spring fresh born from someone's psyche, theories, at least nontrivial theories, do not. Theories are built, destroyed, and revised piecemeal. Theoretical utility and validity come from an interaction between inductive and deductive steps. Sandra Howell offers an analysis of this state of contemporary theory building in these terms:

One of the unfortunate byproducts of this anti-theory attitude is, ironically, production of instant-theory building. Believing that no one is looking back, academics in the environmental design–behavior research arena tend to presume that by naming something a "theory" they have cut a new swath in knowledge. Since few of us bother to publicly criticize such offerings (are we afraid of the awesome note of scholarship embedded in the word "theory"?), the culprits go unconfronted.

Scholarship in Environmental Design must come to be an exchange between inductive (case generated) and deductive (theory generated) process. This is the *pic-up-stix* layering required for the culmination of knowledge that hopefully, will, in fact, be useful to practice.

On Quantification of the Trivial for Confirmation of the Obvious

I know that many readers feel that *Landscape Journal* is dominated by a distinctive segment of our discipline, the fuzzy set, including behavioral investigations, visual assessment, land planning and analysis, and so on, which can be described as quantitative-analytical work. I can almost hear colleagues griping about the *Landscape Research* crowd, or the **** clones (provide your favorite well-known author). I don't know whether this is true or not. Maybe it is something to be treated in a future editorial. But the belief bears on an issue worth discussing.

First, whatever editorial policy this journal has or has not, it cannot be explained by a conspiracy theory. While all the editors of this magazine have had their own personal inclinations and prejudices, I can say with some certainty that they have had little effect on the magazine content. If the types of work mentioned above have been published out of proportion to their role in the discipline or profession it is because the editors have received more of such manuscripts. Authors working within that mode of research have developed the habit of written publications as part of their education and their work. Other sectors of the discipline and the profession have not. But is it possible that the acceptance rate of such papers is higher? Again, I can't say, but I would not be surprised.

People who submit quantitative-analytical manuscripts have usually received doctoral training in their specialized field or, at the very least, have trained extensively under people who have. People who submit quantitative work to this journal have learned to do research. Unfortunately, many of the people who submit "think pieces" have never learned to think. Anyone who takes offense at this harsh characterization should be forced to read some of the drivel submitted under the rubric of design philosophy or theory. There is a corollary to this situation: just as the authors of quantitative work have been trained within an accepted, well-defined paradigm, so have their reviewers. A quantitative research manuscript is easier, or at least cleaner, to evaluate for publication.

The hard fact is that the "humanist" or speculative tradition in landscape architectural scholarship will hold its own with quantitative research in this journal when, and only when, academic landscape architecture programs start teaching their students—and their faculty—the difference between sloppy concern and rigorous thought.

If landscape architecture, and environmental design in general, is the design of settings that functionally support and emotionally enrich the lives of people, then landscape architecture scholarship is the activity that provides the knowledge base for such design. The concept of knowledge base includes not only information but intellectual structures that organize that information: frameworks, models, and, hopefully and eventually, theory. Being a scholarly journal implies the publication of the best in both quantitative research and the so-called humanist tradition. Specifically, this means that our journals should be running more design philosophy, criticism, and, yes, if you will, theory—done with the rigor and clarity of the quantitative work it runs alongside. If indeed there are two separate intellectual currents within our discipline, our journals should be representing the best of each. We could hope that they would begin to inform one another, eventually even affect one another.

Notes

1. This was written some twenty years ago when I was editor of *Landscape Journal*. I have done only a minimum to update or modify it. Some of the villains have changed but the issues persist.

2. I wonder whether the half-life of design-oriented journals or magazines has decreased at a rate comparable to those of the style, heroes, and rhetoric they cover.

3. I was wrong.

♦ ♦ ♦ ♦　About Palimpsests

One of the vogue words recently cycling about in studio and publication is "palimpsest," a referral to the constantly erased and written over parchment of antiquity. Each site is to be a palimpsest for the designer. It's an intriguing idea but I have some questions. First, in the referent world of historians and archaeologists, most palimpsests turn out to be illegible. Finding a palimpsest does not mean that you are reading it correctly, or maybe at all. Still, nominating a site as palimpsest can be a legitimate and worthwhile framework for a designer: a way of working in which various designers can have something in common and still express the individuality of themselves and of particular sites. But there's a big difference between viewing the site as a palimpsest for design inspiration and assuming that it will be read as such by those who use it. Unfortunately, the intent of the designer and experience of the user are not always congruent. Will every site we design have an educational historical booklet provided to explain our intent? Secondly, when does a palimpsest become a litter bin? Has it occurred to us that we're surrounded by palimpsests and don't like them? In the Midwest, at least, every new upscale subdivision has apparently been designed by Laura Ashley: a collage of giant used brick piers to support mailboxes, postmodern cut-out gables and cardboard dormers, nostalgia porches, and corn-husk swags, a palimpsest assemblage approaching terminal nostalgia. If this is a palimpsest, I'll take a Mylar or a print out, thank you. And if history is a palimpsest, then who gets to erase our designs, and how soon?

◢ ◢ ◢ ◢ Speculations on the
New American Landscapes

> Remembrance of a particular form is but regret for a
> particular moment; and houses, roads, avenues are
> as fugitive, alas, as the years.
>
> —Marcel Proust, *Swann's Way*

We know that our landscape has changed remarkably over the last several decades. We sense and see these changes. We dutifully deplore them, and condemn them out of hand as aberrations or threats, or decay to the existing order. We might better look at them as they are, and endeavor to learn from them. While the low-density spread of our cities, for example, has been a major concern of the American media for twenty years, the concurrent development of a new urban pattern, nonhierarchical and multi-noded (Peirce Lewis called it the "galactic city"), has been recognized only by a few. The impact of the strip and then the shopping center has produced many arguments between developers and the purveyors of taste and ecology, but little understanding. Just as some of our new landscapes have been noted and examined, so have some of the forces that have produced them. The rise of mass affluence, leisure, and mobility derived from the automobile, combined with a merchandising economy exploiting them, have been commonly identified, no doubt correctly, as important contributors to new landscape phenomena.

The changes we have recognized have usually been not only deplored but viewed as correctable through better taste and better planning. Our image of the ideal landscape and our relation to it still seems almost capturable by Norman Rockwell, even though the children he pictured skinny-dipping in the creek are probably competing behind the chain-link fence of the local swim club, and their parents fishing in the freeway borrow pit. We see the landscape through filters of custom and taste. We find in it what we seek, for as long as we can, and think of it as the norm.

The many phenomena we see fit together into no obvious pattern. No one theme or clear meaning seems to relate all these changes. Maybe we are too close to them to perceive their relationship. But the phenomena are widespread and distinctive enough to warrant inquiry and interpretation. And if answers elude us, speculation might at least sharpen our questions.

The Pluralistic Landscape

From Timothy Dwight through Toqueville to today, interpreters of the American scene have sought to characterize *the* American landscape—a whole with a distinct national feel. Variations within that landscape have been seen as large homogeneous regions, differing from one another because of the nature of the land, settlement by groups of distinct traditions, or the technological and legal systems guiding their development. The theme of these writers is not only that the American cultural landscape is different from that of other countries but that it or its image (the disentanglement of image from reality being a tricky business) is understandable as one entity, its values and satisfactions shared by most of its inhabitants. This approach has helped us to look at what goes on around us and aided our understanding.

But a useful way to understand what is happening today might be to think about the current American scene, not as one landscape or a few regional ones, but as a pluralistic collection of diverse landscapes created and used by voluntary special-interest groups, each with its own distinctive ways of shaping, using, selling, and perceiving the environment. This might have always been true. The American landscape of the second half of the nineteenth century might be understood as such a collection: the landscapes of the rancher, farmer, railroad, mining town, and so on. Today, however, the role of the landscape as physical resource for specialized interests centered on recreation and merchandising seems to dominate the physical development of the landscape and our attitudes toward it.

This concept of the landscape as a diverse, maybe even centrifugal, collection of independent settings serving special-interest groups has been legitimized and institutionalized through publications and organizations serving its consumers and merchandisers. Proof from the consumer's side is available at any drugstore or supermarket where the magazine racks display *Popular Flyer, Runner's World, Trailer Boats, Treasure Search,* and *Off-Road Travel.* Purveyors can subscribe to *Auto Laundry News, Campground Merchandising, Fast Service* (for managers of drive-ins), *Motel Motor Inn Journal, Shopping Center Digest,* and *Ski Area Management.* Depending on one's landscape preference and role, one can join the Sierra Club, Winnebago International Travelers, North American Family Camping Association, Hotel-Motel Greeters International, International Carwash Council, Conference of National Park Concessioners, or International Drive-In Association. These publications and organizations not only act as pressure groups to promote development of landscapes but define and reinforce specialized attitudes toward the land. Whether this development of specialized landscapes is new or an intensification of an old but little noted trend is less important than the fact that recognition of it could aid our understanding of the contemporary landscape, how people perceive it, and what can and cannot reasonably be expected of it. This way of looking at our landscape is similar to that offered by Nathan Glazer and Daniel Patrick Moynihan in describing our cities as lumpy stews, not melting pots.

New Subcultural Landscapes

The term "cultural landscape" has proven a useful designation for both a phenomenon and a field of study. Perhaps the concept of "subcultural landscape" might also help our understanding of the contemporary environment. It might seem pretentious to apply the term "subculture" to surfers or skimobilers, yet it might offer a new way of looking at our landscapes. If we accept this term, we can immediately distinguish several differences between traditional and contemporary subcultures.

Traditional subcultures were distinguished by at least three features: participation in them was relatively unexamined; membership was normally long-term, maybe lifelong; and their forms were determined by tradition—regional, ethnic, or both. That some people did examine them and leave them only strengthens the claim for their stability and required commitment, because the pain of such examination and breaking free has been a major theme in our literature. Subcultures often produced their own distinct landscapes, whether the Cajun parishes of Louisiana or the Spanish uplands of northern New Mexico.

Today membership in subcultures is often a conscious selection by the participant, sometimes independent of class or job. Participation no longer need be lifelong; commitment is sometimes associated with a phase of life or personal development and in extreme cases may be only for weekends. Lastly, the forms through which such a subculture expresses itself and confirms its identity seldom stem directly from regional or social traditions; they are likely to be innovations or borrowings from remote times and places.

Whether or not we apply the term subculture to contemporary lifestyles, the exercise points up differences between the social associations that formerly shaped our landscape and those that shape it today. Contemporary subcultures can be seen as popular, or mass, cultures and their older counterparts as folk cultures. Folk cultures are stable and conservative, with products derived from tradition. Popular cultures are changeable, with forms derived from the media. These distinctions can also be applied to the buildings and landscapes created or used by subcultures.

Our landscape is undergoing what has been called "massification." This has already happened to our media, popular literature, and ways of building. The landscape—stable, difficult, and slow to change—is one of the last parts of society to reflect the dominance of mass culture, but it is finally yielding. The landscape produced is as pluralistic as contemporary mass culture itself. The massification of our landscape has not gone unnoted, but it, too, has been thought an aberration, a commercial connivance to be deplored and if possible stopped. It is, instead, a logical and perhaps inevitable expression of our society. It can be deplored, but short of a drastic change in our society, it is no more likely to be stopped or reversed than the spread of television. Henry Glassie has made a useful distinction between mass and folk culture, arguing that "folk material exhibits major variation over space and minor variation through time, while the products of popular culture exhibit minor variations over space and major variation through time. . . . a search for patterns in folk material yields regions, where a search for patterns in popular material yields periods."

This observation reveals two more ways new landscapes differ from traditional ones. The first is more rapid change. Change is not easy to live with, but if accelerated change is an integral part of mass culture we must take it as the rule and not an aberration. The hope that the ordinary landscape, laden with cultural and personal memories, might serve as a stable reference against future shock is forlorn. Attempts at preservation of the cultural landscape, a fashionable topic on the conference circuit, may produce only museum pieces or tourist attractions.

The second difference between old and new landscapes implied in Glassie's statement lies in their spatial pattern. A mass landscape will not produce those large homogeneous regions, distinct one from the other, that characterized folk culture. Just as most new subcultures are, or quickly become, national, so do their landscapes. This supposed homogenization of the American landscape disturbs the sophisticated commentators of the mass media. To be sure, we can travel through space but not time. A distant landscape can be revisited; a past landscape cannot, theme parks not withstanding. Why is temporal change frightening but areal change admired? This supposed homogenization deserves to be questioned. Given the diversity and fragmentation of current mass culture, the difference between old and new landscapes might lie not in the amount of diversity but in its pattern, specifically in its grain. Writers repeatedly claim that our cities look more and more alike, as in Calvin Trillin's worries over the "Houstonization" of New Orleans. What has not been considered, however, is that New Orleans, Houston, and most of our contemporary cities might contain more diverse landscapes within them than ever before. Do our new landscapes really lack diversity, or has their diversity gone unrecognized because it occurs in a finer pattern and at a smaller scale?

A new historic consciousness among designers and the liberal political elite is producing the preservation of fragments of the traditional urban scene and restoring entire neighborhoods. The development of landscapes as diverse as new suburbs, office and apartment complexes lining circumferential freeways, strips and shopping centers, and even, as Grady Clay has noted, the penetration of the landscape of pornography into suburbia, makes it hard to justify describing our cities as less diverse than those of three decades ago. Diversity is a subjective term. Observers of the landscape apply it mostly to differences traceable to folk traditions of regional or ethnic origin, which are supposedly less self-conscious than those of mass culture. As Glassie noted, a typology that depends on this distinction is of little use today, when it is impossible for a genuine folk article to be produced in an unreflective manner. Ian Nairn, an advocate of diversity based on place, said it well: "Making a pattern out of the environment has got to be conscious—the days when it would come naturally are long past. Somehow, though, differences derived from conscious design, whether popular or elite, are assumed to be less real than those of folk tradition, and their diversity continues unnoticed or is dismissed as 'plastic.'"

A good metaphor for the older American landscape might be a quilt made from a few pieces of solid, bright colors, clearly different and demarcated. That newer landscape might be intricately designed, mass-produced wallpaper, in which elements are repeated all across the country, but exist in propinquity and great variety at a smaller scale. The diversity of the wallpaper is not less than the diversity of the quilt—only different.

Packaged Landscapes

Just as the stability, cultural typology, and spatial pattern of our landscape have changed, so have its forms, uses, and control. These changes can be seen most clearly by looking at the most popular landscapes, rather than at landscapes traditionally thought important, or landscapes that fit conventional aesthetic or social values. Mass use of a landscape might only be a choice among inadequate alternatives, not the satisfaction of deep human needs, but our knowledge of needs and satisfaction from the landscape is now minimal. The most visible and superficially successful landscapes, as judged on their prevalence and popularity, are a good place to start. Many of our most popular, heavily used landscapes and many of the developments distinguishing our landscape from that of thirty years ago are commercial. They can be characterized as landscapes that are openly merchandised, landscapes in which the distinction between public and private is blurred, and landscapes in which management dominates design.

Given the dominant commercial orientation of our society over the last three decades, the extent and visibility of the commercial landscape is not surprising. But as such landscapes have spread, they have taken on a new role. They have become competitive merchandising tools and shapers of commercial images—total packages, for sale or hire. The merchandising techniques of Disney World and other theme parks have trickled down to "destination" and "resort" campgrounds where up to 70 percent of gross revenue comes from "profit centers" such as stores, game rooms, and waterslides, not from site rentals. Housing developments are promoted as "total environments" with a distinctive image, be it quaint or cosmopolitan—an approach far more comprehensive than the older habit of taking street names from Walter Scott novels. Newer shopping malls offer a similar package to their customers. The space in front of McDonald's restaurants, where parking space has yielded to token tables and chairs, has now evolved into "McDonald Land." John Portman and his imitators have returned to the hotel tradition of monumental space, which had been eliminated in the motels of the 1950s and '60s. In its most elaborate examples this space approaches a total interior landscape, closer in spirit to the Victorian conservatory than to modern approaches of framing the exterior landscape or dissolving barriers between outside and inside. It rejects the exterior landscape, which is usually devoted to cars, the disarray of the strip, and the decay of the downtown. In its ultimate expressions it makes that rejection, and the abnegation of public responsibility, visually explicit through the use of mirrored glass walls.

As lavish commercial settings evolve into total landscapes, the legal, spatial, and perceptual distinctions between public and private space become more difficult to define. The landscapes of the past were one or the other; the differences between the great estate and the park, courthouse square, or business street were clear. As people entered a store, they clearly moved from one realm to the other. But theme parks, KOAs, and malls seem neither public nor private but proprietary spaces that contain aspects of each, where traditional distinctions mean little.

Maybe the change began on the strip. There we knew that the highway was public and the interior of the restaurant or liquor store was private (at least we were there at the owner's sufferance). But how did we perceive the auto-serving spaces in between? The land was in private title, but the parking lot cruising of the 1950s was as public as any Italian *passeggiata*. The ambitiously landscaped corporate office park abutting the interstate highway is private land, but it is perceived, and probably meant to be perceived, as a public amenity. The enclosed shopping mall transcends purely commercial activity to usurp former functions of public space; the Girl Scout concert and the community art show are held there, and Planned Parenthood competes with Right-to-Life for bake sale dollars. The right to distribute literature in shopping centers, on the grounds that they constitute public space, has been the subject of at least one court case. Sliding shop fronts dissipate the barrier between individual stores and circulation space in the mall, McDonald's lures school groups to its playgrounds, and each weekend thousands of Americans contribute to the growth of proprietary space as they open their garage doors to sell the family's castoffs.

These commercial landscapes seem determined less by principles of design than of management. This distinction is almost as difficult to make as spatial definitions on the strip, but there is still a difference. One is that design determines and management responds. Design can convey many values, while management is dominated by only one—efficiency. Certainly a mark of shopping center management is its pragmatism and responsiveness to change, expressed in its decision to lease or refuse space, and its control over the decoration of such space. Dominance of management over design or uncontrolled experience is not limited to commercial landscapes—witness the federal government's concern with "visual management" as a guideline for development of public lands.

Do these packaged landscapes serve people's needs any better or worse than parks and courthouse squares once did? There are no nineteenth-century user-satisfaction studies of parks to compare with those that could be compiled for today's shopping centers. Does the often-noted absence of sleeping winos in suburban shopping malls really mean that those spaces are not successful environments? There might be a difference between what consumers want and what society needs, but who defines that difference?

It does not require a Marxist landscape critic to be uneasy about the fact that our most successful communal spaces are neither created nor controlled by any communal body. Maybe the profit-oriented management of the new landscapes is as attentive to its users' wants as were the builders of the nineteenth-century railroad palaces or the politicians who supported the great turn-of-the-century urban park systems. Maybe the consumer's legendary discretionary dollar is as effective in achieving responsive landscapes as a vote for park commissioner once was. But however cynical and rapacious the political system underlying the City Beautiful movement might have been, it never claimed that all the goals of an Olmsted park system were summed up in a profit and loss statement. In the end, no one is a citizen of Six Flags Over Texas.

A New Urbanity?

The strong antiurban bias of American culture has been a persistent theme among observers of our society and our landscape, as most convincingly documented in the writings of Morton and Lucia White. Yet for three decades the media has assured us that urban revitalization is just around the corner. The centralization of the media in our larger cities (the rare exception is *Reader's Digest,* which might have invented Pleasantville, New York, if it hadn't discovered it) and its staffing by young people attracted by the urban image may have produced a media message masking the fact that most Americans care no more about the city, except as an unwanted sink for their tax money, than they ever did.

This bias might partially explain the fate of older urban renewal schemes that so often inserted great open spaces into languishing central business districts. The schemes began with skillful public relations renderings of big-city plazas containing more trees than all the squares of Europe, and from there filtered down through increasingly drab, unimaginative street-to-mall conversions in ever-smaller cities. Those spaces almost never fulfilled their promise of attracting new business or public life. Their emptiness is one of the saddest sights of our contemporary landscape.

But things seem different today. The renewed area around Boston's Fanueil Hall draws more visitors in a year than Disney World, a comparative measure of success that seems to surprise no one. Novelty, the long local romance with history, exceptionally sensitive planning and design—any of these might make Boston an unusual case. Still, what is happening there and in other cities is not the indifference that greeted the plazas of the 1960s, nor, so far, the brief popularity and subsequent slide into seediness or squalor of Underground Atlanta, Gaslight Square in St. Louis, or Chicago's Old Town. The spreading rehabilitation of older urban housing also seems evidence of a change in attitudes toward the city. If the complex financial role of the federal government disqualifies such redevelopment as pure free-market choice, nevertheless there seems a message of change since the days of renewal by fiat and bulldozer. And if it is primarily the professional and managerial elite, and the upwardly ambitious young who are vitalizing the city, well—who led that original movement to the suburbs?

What might be causing this shift in values? One answer is that the suburban dream has faded, that families who might once have moved to suburbia now find it wanting on the same counts on which designers and sociologists have long faulted it—automobile dependence, long commutes, social pressure, and a bland, homogeneous life and setting.

Karl Meyer offers a more cynical interpretation, observing that in 1958 eight of ten most-watched U.S. television shows were laid in rural or Old West settings, while in 1975 eight of ten were laid in urban or big city suburban settings—a "long march from hitching post to corner drug store to mean streets." He sees this change, and the boom in urban sports and culture, not as a response to new cultural values, but as the product of a media marketing strategy that packages audiences into metropolitan units.

But there is another possible answer that would mark a deeper change in attitudes. The suburbs were merchandised not only as meeting an American "need" for owning a single-family, detached house on plenty of land but as the ideal setting for a particular model of family life—a model in which the man was the absent-five-days-a-week income producer and the occasional weekend handyman, and the woman the manager of house, family, and civic activities. How effectively the suburban setting physically supported such activity is an open question, but the images of environment and family were linked. Increasing numbers of young middle-class people, particularly women, seem to reject that model of family life, and they might well be a major source of the people refurbishing older parts of our cities. The interest in the city might be less a preference for the traditional urban amenities than for the greater practical facility with which the city supports the life of a family, perhaps childless, in which two adults work outside the home and allot their other roles in accord with individual preferences and needs, not traditional sex roles.

Changes also seem to be occurring in the use of public space and in the image of urbanity. We have learned, finally, that physical design, although it can impede or suppress positive use of a space, seldom generates it. Candid designers point to the role of programmed, well-funded, formal activities as a major generator of such use, and their absence as a serious obstacle. A great deal of the less structured use of such spaces centers on luxurious, conspicuous consumption—patronage of boutiques, poster and furnishings shops, and purveyors expensive and exotic foods. (Everyone seems to be buying this food or eating it on the spot; who could have foreseen pushcart entrepreneurs selling quiche in that northernmost bastion of southern cooking, Washington, D.C.?) Management and merchandising seem as dominant in the new urban street life as in the suburban shopping mall. Successful and active as that street life might be, it is not the same mix of activities associated with the traditional *passeggiata*, or hanging out or promenading. If the support that cities offer to freer family organization raises high hopes for a new urbanism, the dependence of street life on public funding and luxury retailing also raises questions for the future.

Before the Second World War, the tastemaker's image of American urbanity emphasized elegance: tree-filled parks and boulevards, Beaux-Arts opera houses, and uniformed doormen beneath cast-iron porte cocheres. Today the city is increasingly viewed as a place for excitement, not elegance. The essence of urbanity is seen, not as an ordered setting for decorous display of wealth and class distinction, but as a chaotic bazaar offering the expense-account and "conferences" society an eclectic and hedonistic assortment of delights ranging from Scandinavian furniture to Szechuan cooking. This is a change from tony to trendy, even to tawdry. If the image is still European, it is that of Montmartre, not the Champs-Élysées. It is a change Roger Starr characterized well in his comparison of sauce Béarnaise to the chicken on the delicatessen rotisserie, a change highlighted in the contemporary advertisement of a Volvo parked in front of a graffiti-covered wall—a safe exposure to delights that border on the dangerous, "a civilized car for an uncivilized world." Like the success of new spaces, the success of this new image is often tied to spending and acquisition.

The Landscape of Nostalgia

Nostalgia is not a new element in human appreciation of the landscape. It dates back at least to late Roman times, as David Lowenthal has noted. Its omnipresence as a merchandisable commodity, however, is a vivid but discouraging aspect of our contemporary landscape. The landscape of nostalgia is not the use of historic forms or references by elite architects, as in the Renaissance or the revivals of the nineteenth century. It is not the contextualism of today's avant-garde, nor the obeisance to genius loci of the Townscape school. Neither is it the desire to maintain a visual sense of history and continuity in our urban fabric, nor the desire to conserve building shells of the past for present reuse, whether for visual rationales or energy conservation reasons.

The landscape of nostalgia, although sometimes difficult to separate from such approaches, is an attempt to re-create physically an environment of saccharine comfort associated with a past life thought simpler and more reassuring than today's. Fred Davis defined nostalgia as applying only to events or objects that an individual has experienced personally, limiting the time span to one's own life. This definition seems too narrow—times that we were told about by parents and grandparents, for example, surely can be a part of our emotional life. Lowenthal has even noted a commercial restoration based on this, where everything is continually arranged to appear seventy-five years old. If the goal of nostalgia is successful escape, then its landscape should represent a time and place recapturable in the imagination, but the success of Disney World's Main Street might indicate that clever manipulation can extend that time back further, maybe all the way to Old Sturbridge.

As the element of nostalgia in our relation to the landscape is not new, neither are attempts to design landscapes of nostalgia, such as the rural pastiches at Versailles. But traditionally such designs were limited to creations for the very rich, to special museum settings such as "Yesteryear's Main Street," or, more recently, to the landscape of tourism. Today it is a mass phenomenon. We can enter a taxi in almost any large American city and confidently ask to be taken to the local renewed nineteenth-century warehouse district where we find the expected decor of macramé, butcher block, and exposed brick known in the trade as "fern bar" style. Housing magazines advise developers to "cash in on today's wave of nostalgia with early American design. And make the design authentic." In Mystic, Connecticut, we can shop in Olde Mistick Village shopping center, built from scratch in 1976 to resemble what we imagine as a New England village of 1720 (sanitized, of course). We need tolerance and a willingness to suspend value judgments to understand our contemporary landscape, which often violates traditional canons of taste and beauty. But the widespread commercial reconstruction of landscapes that we never knew but wish we had is troubling. It seems to show not only that our relations with the contemporary landscape are unsatisfying but that we are reluctant to confront that fact. Occasional fantasy, whether Stockbroker Tudor or Disney Main Street, is one thing; the routine substitution of fantasy for reality in the everyday environment, and the willing confusion of which is which, are another matter.

Hedonism, High Technology, and Encapsulation

The American romance with technology has been a long one. Leo Marx saw it personified in Benjamin Franklin and illustrated by the locomotives and steamboats in nineteenth-century landscape paintings. But since Thoreau pondered the railroad whistle sounding in the countryside, technology has not only increased the power and speed offered to its user but has become available to the individual, not just the community, in the form of automobiles, power boats, and recreational and off-road vehicles. As technology has become more personalized, it has become more flexible, more capable of conquering place and terrain, and has come to offer a variety of immediate, personal gratifications. The image of technology and power over nature embodied in the train or steamboat was abstract compared to the feel of a trail bike under hands and feet.

Sensory delight in speed, motion, and impact, control over our movement and over brute technological power, and mastery over the environment are themes in many contemporary involvements with the landscape. The theme is seen in the new roller coaster mania, in the musical romanticization of the trucker's landscape, and even in the use of the power mower, which has so drastically changed the grounds of the farmstead. Some of the newly popular activities—soaring, hang gliding, downhill skiing, surfing, skateboarding, roller-skating, and watersliding, and other extreme sports—depend on highly sophisticated technology. Even backpacking has developed its own folding aluminum, high-technology, imported camping-gear syndrome. High technology has become an object of fascination as important as the experience it serves. The confining upper-class dress and the formalized rhythmic body movement of the eighteenth century—the farthingale and slipper, the polonaise, the thrust and parry of fencing—were seen by Steen Eiler Rasmussen in *Experiencing Architecture* as reflections of the great baroque systems of channeled, sequential movement and attendant conceptions of space and landscape. Perhaps the eclectically costumed skier or roller skater, speeding through the landscape wearing radio headphones, could tell us something about the role and image of our contemporary environment, if we only knew what to ask.

The popularity of mobile, miniaturized, encapsulated environments— the trailer, motor home, pickup camper, and van—is a complementary development. It might be unnecessary to search for deep psychic motivations behind this, because simple convenience explains much of it. Still, it is not hard to see evidence of territoriality in the physical structuring of a defensible home territory portable through a strange environment. Nor is it difficult to see evidence of the aedicular complex described by Summerson in *Heavenly Mansions* and by Moore and his coauthors in *The Place of Houses* in the miniaturization of the suburban interior in mobile homes, or the fantasy pleasure palace in Tijuana-baroque van decor, and of rustic butcher block in the truck houses of the Bay Area. Or perhaps the owners of these encapsulated environments are acting out Leo Marx's and science fiction's theme of retreat, exploration, and return, condensed in time and space, with the motor home serving as city and the dirt-bike trail as wilderness.

But whatever human drives might be at work, one aspect of their relationship with the environment has been given little thought. The litter and visual intrusion, the damage and even destruction associated with these mobile dwellings, are thought to show a contemptuous disregard for the environment by the users. But these people might simply have a different concept of their environment than do managers and backpackers. To these recreationists, the mobile dwelling might be the essential environment, with the casually visited, interchangeable, exterior physical setting becoming a simple resource of convenience. Care and emotional involvement are encouraged by long exposure through time and enriched by successive discovery. When landscapes become only transient, interchangeable settings, deeper relationships may be missing. The encapsulated environment, not the landscape, receives care and offers emotional meaning, perhaps just as garden and farmstead once did.

Scarcity of gasoline and the rise in its price will undoubtedly affect the use of these motorized, miniaturized environments, but it is not certain that it will significantly reduce their popularity. In the great gasoline shortage of the 1970s, the 1978 per capita petroleum consumption in California, that supposed source and symbol of nomadic, irresponsible lifestyle, was only 0.3 percent greater than the national average. This indicates that recreational-vehicle use could well survive energy restrictions. Campground owners observed that in the summer of 1979, although use of remote campgrounds dropped severely, those nearer large population centers preserved or even increased their occupancy rates—another measure of the importance and adaptability of this phenomenon. The pollution, land damage, and energy investment involved in this new definition of environment are real. But unless we understand that spontaneity, sensual pleasure, and a longstanding fondness for technology, and a flexible concept of environment, are not transitory fads or consumer gimmicks, but evolving ways of relating to the landscape, we shall not find effective ways of reducing their impact.

The Withering of Class

Many of our older landscapes were associated with social class distinctions.[1] The elite of nineteenth-century American cities congregated on tree-lined boulevards and park roads, just as the baroque aristocracy gathered in monumental avenues and plazas. The country clubs surrounding American cities were once landscapes of social class—archetypal settings for the works of F. Scott Fitzgerald and John O'Hara, just as the streets and pool halls of the city were for James T. Farrell. The rituals of the croquet green or tennis court differed from those of the soccer field or baseball diamond in accordance with differences in social status. Today such distinctions still exist, but they are so finely drawn or restricted to so few settings as to offer little help in understanding our landscape. The role of landscape in reinforcing class distinctions, in confirming who or where you were on the social ladder, was perhaps a positive role only for those at the top. Still, the loss of that role eliminates one more source of continuity and one more stable relationship with the landscape.

Problems and Portents

The derivation of our landscape forms from the media rather than tradition; the loss of homogeneous regional character, and its replacement by variation over time; the role of special-interest groups and voluntary associations; the provision, control, and ownership of landscapes by corporations rather than communities; the loss of public-private demarcation and ties to social class—although these themes fit no simple pattern and their meaning might be unclear, they at least allow some general observations on our relationship to the contemporary landscape and that of the near future. One is that many traditional relationships that gave meaning to the landscape are no longer tenable. Often our relationship with the landscape now is that of visitors to places of which we neither have nor need deep, intimate knowledge. Theme parks, national parks, and urban malls for the weekend visitor are removed in space and time from much of daily life. Even today's farmer might need a more detailed knowledge of equipment, chemicals, and tax strategies than of his land, which becomes, like the desert setting for visiting trail bikers, another interchangeable resource of convenience. Our settings are provided already packaged by others. We have little involvement and few ties with these settings: no ownership, no control, little or no legal or emotional responsibility. Our satisfactions derive not from pride of ownership or development, nor from emotional tie to place, nor from tradition. They are, instead, sensory and transient—eating, racing, viewing, buying and selling—the satisfactions not of builders or participants but of quick consumers. Perhaps these relationships are not less satisfying than older ones, only different. Perhaps they are a first stage in the development of new relationships.

Another discouraging aspect of our new landscapes is that the burden of forging new, meaningful relationships falls on the individual or the isolated family, with little help from tradition or other people. If this is a freedom, it is a lonely one. Many activities pursued so fervently in our landscape—the buying and selling of expensive bric-a-brac, the hedonistic quick fix abetted by technology, the attachment to the luxurious encapsulated environment, the constant movement—could be interpreted as a troubled search for ties, meaning, and involvement. Perhaps they portray a landscape of alienation—that specter hinted at in the ironic humor of Calvin Trillin and sketched with frightening immediacy in recent essays by Herbert Gold, William Kowinski, and Michael Harrington. We know too little about the role landscapes play in satisfying psychic needs to make easy characterizations. Still, there is a sadness in the spectacle of millions of isolated individuals, J. B. Priestley's "Nomadmass," making their lonely way across the landscape, seeking vestiges of communal participation through transitory groupings like trailer-club meetings, van-ins, or what Grady Clay called "swarming," all engaged in a search for pleasure in temporary, almost interchangeable landscapes.

Human adaptability is considerable. If current relationships with landscapes seem superficial compared to those available in the past, that does not mean deeper relationships cannot again be developed. But optimism should not come easily. Adaptation takes time. Given the transient nature of forms derived from mass culture and the even more rapid change associated with hyped-up commercialism, we might find ourselves always struggling to adapt to yesterday's landscapes. The issue is not whether we can adapt to new environments, but what physiological and psychological costs such adaptation requires. The term "adaptation" carries a connotation of tolerating an environment without incurring excessive stress. Is the best we can expect from our future environment the absence of harmful stress rather than the deeper meanings possible in the past? If adaptation takes more time than we have, what are our chances for developing enduring satisfaction?

If the quickening pace of change raises troubling doubts, so does the fact that our landscapes are increasingly provided, owned, and managed by bureaucracies or corporations such as the Bureau of Land Management and the Marriott Corporation—organizations remote from our daily life, and control. Our only power to affect such landscapes is withholding our dollars, a negative influence more likely to eliminate unsatisfactory landscapes than to shape fulfilling ones. Our feeling of control over the environment and our sense of competence can be as important as the attributes of the environment itself. That feeling of control is not likely to be significant in a bureaucratically or corporately managed environment.

Finally, the commercial nature of many of our new landscapes raises doubts about their future in an increasingly precarious economy. Equating success with earnings is not confined to commercial landscapes; federal and state campgrounds, for example, are under pressure to raise prices to reduce operating losses in a time of taxpayer discontent and to respond to complaints of unfair competition and hidden subsidies raised by private operators. The high capital and maintenance investment of packaged environments requires those environments to return a profit. If profits fail, will we see a landscape littered with the evidence of unsuccessful competitors, or will HUD money revitalize theme parks and motel pleasure domes? Travel and sophisticated personal technology require affluent consumers; our new landscapes are built not only on leisure but on well-moneyed leisure. Much of the success of shopping centers and urban malls depends on buying and selling—not merchandising staple goods in bazaars or crossroads grocery stores of the past, but purveying luxury items. We might choose to stroll rather than to buy, but unless someone is buying posters, quiche, and lattes, these settings may not survive. The possibility of an economic depression, more than energy costs, raises doubts about the long-term viability of many of our new landscapes.

We are faced with forgoing older relationships with our landscape and forging new ones, with little help from tradition or community, in times of faster change and decreasing individual control. Some satisfactions sought in the landscape still depend on stable, long-enduring relationships. Those satisfactions may be ever harder to find. The sadness and pain of change are part of the human experience; the stability and continuity of the landscape as a counterbalance would be no small gift for troubled lives. If earth abides forever, packaged landscapes do not. Troubling environmental problems of the years ahead will include not only conserving energy and protecting natural systems but also emotionally coping with a landscape more transitory than we have ever experienced, more than Proust could have envisioned.

Note

1. Class as I used it here must be distinguished from wealth. Certainly, ostentatious display of the latter has increased manyfold since this was written, and has become a prominent marker of our new landscape. The spread of the gated community (which obviously I did not see coming) probably serves both functions.

⫻ ⫻ ⫻ ⫻ Vision, Culture, and Landscape

At first cut, and in the end, there are two basic and different ways of addressing the landscape experience. The issue is drawn between those who approach the landscape as a figural composition, as a picture, versus those who study the landscape as a social phenomenon. The social characterization is the less successful because at least two different approaches are subsumed under it, a point to which I'll return. There is also the issue that a pictorial composition can be investigated primarily as a socioeconomic product, indeed that seems the current fashion in art history, but that can be worried about when we are much further along in our intellectual sophistication about actual perception of and reaction to the landscape. This distinction is more an artifact of human analysis than of the experience itself. This split has a historic precedent. Denis Cosgrove, for example, has associated the pictorial/experienced landscape dichotomy with the rise of capitalism and the appropriation of land, in contrast to the feudal system. Whatever its relation to the real ongoing world, the split characterizes the two dominant academic subcultures that currently deal with the landscape.

Why these two particular attitudes? Where do they come from and why? A bit of the cultural materialist analysis that some of the younger British historians have brought to bear upon the entire landscape tradition can profitably be applied to our own immediate situation. The sociology of the design discipline and profession should clarify not only the context of this dichotomy but the dichotomy itself.

Why did the visual assessment movement, which dates to the work of Kenneth Craik in the early 1970s, take off so suddenly to dominate the quantitative wing and much of the literature of landscape analysis? First, being based on the model of bench science, it served as a wonderful banner for reaction against intuition in design. It gave us a claim to membership in the "scientific" paradigm that swept U.S. academia in the aftermath of the Manhattan Project. Second, it involved, if only in a second- or thirdhand way, the belief in populism and participation of the late 1960s and early '70s. Third, much of its success within the discipline is because it presents such a clear, definable, understandable paradigm. As an editor, I can say that whatever the limitations of the typical visual analysis study, the fact is that the model is clear enough, and the school of followers identifiable enough, that it is quite easy to criticize and review with confidence.

Equally important, the movement served the purposes of powerful outside patrons—government funding agencies. This was a model that they could use to serve and to justify their own goals. One does not have to believe in conspiracy theory to admit this point. The question, then, is to what degree the visual assessment movement asks those questions the answers to which will increase our understanding of the experience of landscape, and to what extent it is a response to a combination of available tools (e.g., statistical analysis and computer technologies), users, and funding agencies.

The situation in the other camp—the "cultural landscape" people, whoever they are—is not at all so easily explained by sociohistoric generalizations. Many of the cultural landscape studies that we see today are a continuation of long traditions of landscape studies going back as far as Carl Sauer at Berkeley, and maybe further back, to the French regional geographers. The resurgence of it might be explained as partly an academic, humanist reaction to the neo-scientist school. But if much is analyzable in hindsight, some things are not. The role of J. B. Jackson in catalyzing this movement could not have been predicted from any historical analysis. Peirce Lewis, Wilber Zelinsky, and others would have done their work with or without Jackson. But he brought the designers into the camp. For most of the last few decades, cultural landscape studies have been proportionately more popular, if more superficial, in design schools than in geography departments.

This split is not inherent in the subject, but it is not illogical. The question is whether such an admittedly artificial dichotomy, isolating and highlighting the pictorial and the social aspects of the landscape, serves, or can serve, a useful purpose in increasing our understanding. I think it can, for reasons that I will come to.

Some characteristics of the pictorial approach, long exemplified by visual assessment, help focus these issues. First, visual assessment is purely, entirely, visual and pictorial. It deals with visual patterns, values, and composition. Second, visual assessment deals with a spatially static landscape. It is not a landscape through which a person moves, nor currently a landscape which itself changes. Third, the landscape is framed and is isolated from the observer, who is not a physical participant. Fourth, the experience itself lacks a temporal dimension. Judgments are made not about an ongoing continuing experience but about a one-off stimulus and appraisal. (Practitioners of this method do not explicitly claim that these constraints, and particularly the history of the individual, are irrelevant, but they are not a factor in their work.)

These assumptions and limitations might seem to make visual assessment of little worth. But the issue of the role of the sponsors or patrons is important. My characterization of assumptions implicit in visual assessment thoroughly describes, for example, the experience of someone touring a national park with a camera. Therefore, prima facie, the method should be an excellent one for locating a scenic overlook on a national park road. And this is, of course, one of its uses, as well as managing the landscape scene to be photographed from that overlook.

However, typical content analysis associated with the visual assessment movement too often goes beyond analysis of preferences and overreaches itself to assert generalizations that claim to advance our understanding of beauty in the landscape. Ah . . . imagine Henry Hoare the younger excitedly writing William Kent to inform him that, having shown watercolor sketches to all the literate villagers in the country, he has found an overwhelming preference for still water in the middle foreground, preferably right of center, in landscapes? Imagine Van Gogh excitedly writing to Gauguin, telling him that, having shown his sketches to all his friends, he has found that over 80 percent of them prefer an area roughly equal to 10 percent of the total canvas area, located slightly lower left of the picture center, to be saturated chrome yellow? Paul, writing back, tactfully reminds Vincent that his sample consists of fellow inmates of a mental institution and might not be accepted as a statistically valid representation of the larger picture-viewing population. Might Paul (having gotten past the local human subjects in research board) have tried the same experiment with his Tahitian friends, to determine whether cross-cultural generalizations could be made?

In the end, reactions to landscapes are assumed essentially the same as "the gallery experience" of looking at a landscape painting, thus dismissing in one stroke the whole issue of the relationship between landscape painting and the landscape itself. After all, Gertrude Jekyll herself said that a garden should have the same effect as a beautiful picture.

Current pictorial analysis brings to mind the almost two-centuries-long debate embedded at the core of our own Anglo-American landscape tradition: that voluminous critical literature generated from the Augustans through Ruskin and Hamerton almost two centuries later. This rich, long, intellectual debate about landscape as picture and picture as landscape seems to have been totally ignored in discussion about the visual assessment movement. I can think of no more severe indictment of the shallowness and lack of grounding in the current state of our discipline than this omission.

There are major, significant differences between those older investigations and contemporary visual analysis. There are three concerns of great importance to the older debate but missing from ours. First is the concern with the substantive content or message of the landscape and particularly with its referents, allusions, and symbols. Second, in nineteenth-century discussions of landscape painting there was intense concern with the dynamics, the evanescence, of the landscape as an important part of the experience, perhaps even the core of that experience. Think of Constable's clouds, Turner's fire and storms. The painter's paramount interest was the ability to capture, and the necessity to understand, the impact of those changes in the landscape that gave it both its character and its impact upon the beholder. Third, there was concern, often a primary interest, in the *mood* produced by a landscape or a landscape painting. To Ruskin, the core of the problem was what we today might call the affective impact on the viewer. This was occasionally taken even further, in ways that psychologists of a century later find embarrassing, to the concept of landscape personality types thought to correspond with certain classes of landscapes.

The participants or actors differ as well; those differences are simple and striking. Contemporary work consists of "objective" observers dealing with lay participants. One aim is to see if it is possible to scientifically arrive at a consensus of lay opinion that crosses lines of class, occupation, gender, and age. In the older debate, the actors were all themselves philosophers or doers, without pretense of "objectivity." They aimed at a consensus, not of the masses, but of connoisseurs. The contemporary work is descriptive; the older was discursive.

The comparison between such older work and today raises some issues. First, if we are to deal with the landscape as a picture, as visual assessment does, we should push that line of inquiry as far as we can. We should try to be as sophisticated and comprehensive as we are able. That's what the older generations did that we are not doing. If the landscape is a picture, we should be dealing beyond the visual content, with its changeability and dynamics, and with its affective impact beyond preference, or "mood," if you wish. Second, expanding the pictorial inquiry into these issues begins to bridge the gap between the pictorial and that other area loosely characterized as the social aspects of the landscape experience. Third, we are designers and scholars. But are we leaders or market analysts?

Are there other dichotomies that might well be as productive in broadening or deepening our understanding of the landscape experience? With the caveat that all such dichotomies are artificial but potentially useful, consider the immediately experienced landscape versus the recalled, the internal landscape versus the external, the individual landscape versus the communal, the insider's landscape versus the outsider's, the spurious landscape versus the real, and finally, the aesthetic landscape versus the utilitarian or ordinary. I'll leave these for now to return later.

Might the pictorial landscape essentially be only a cuing device? It would be useful to explore this possible role. Are all landscapes first experienced as a pattern, visual gestalt, or a "picture"? (I will not raise the "does affect precede cognition" debate here.) We all have felt how different the landscape experience is after even a few hours' exposure to it than when we first encountered it. Might the pictorial landscape usefully be thought of as a threshold or barrier that we must move beyond before the landscape can accumulate any other content? If the pictorial landscape is first threshold, then organized entry into the mental, emotional filing system, is it also both the classifying and retrieving device? Is the pictorial landscape just a means to an end? The rare exceptions would then be particularly interesting.

A world of cultural content lurks behind those preferential judgments. What are we "measuring" when we test for "preference"? Surely there is a cultural bias at some level of abstraction. To take the question to its extreme, are landscapes "preferred" to the degree to which they approach some Platonic essence, a culturally determined mythic landscape? Are the Monument Valley of John Wayne and the Manhattan of Fred Astaire or Woody Allen examples of such cultural essences?

To what degree are preference judgments based on internal landscape narratives? How much do we really know about what goes on inside a person's head when he or she prefers/selects some landscape photographs rather than others? Is that the person fantasizing himself or herself into that landscape, internally playacting a role within that setting? A scenic overlook or an 8 × 10 photograph may be a nonparticipatory experience physically, but we don't know what it is emotionally. Is the reviewer evaluating not only a mythic landscape but also his or her role in it? Do fantasies of John Wayne figure in every male American's evaluation of photographs of the American West? Does fantasy reinforce culture in determining preference?

We know almost nothing about the relationship between the pictorial and other aspects of the landscape experience. Is it, for example, temporally stable? Likely not, and a changing balance between the visual landscape image and all other aspects of the experience may be the hallmark of our times. It is most unlikely that the role of the visual landscape image under a global, high-technology, communication/information image society is the same as that in a preliterate culture, or the high-literate culture of the eighteenth and nineteenth centuries. The classic distinction, made by William James and extensively quoted since, between the insider's and the outsider's landscape is becoming less and less clear, and less and less meaningful in our life. It also, I think, discredits for the same reason Ted Relph's distinction between spurious landscapes and real landscapes. When almost all landscapes are affected by the media, what is spurious and what is "real"? MTV must be telling us something. I am not sure what it is, or whether I want to know.

We need to replace that visual/cultural dichotomy with a less simplistic and restrictive paradigm. Consider a possible four-part schema. The first part would be the pictorial. Second, studies of the "cultural landscape" fall into two different areas, worked on by two distinct academic subcultures. One investigates the landscape as cultural artifact. The other studies the landscape as a setting for social interaction. One group studies the evolution of the landscape, the other its use and perception. Even within those who study the landscape as social phenomenon there are now two blatantly different subcultures. One might be called the "design behavior group," a loose association that for some began in Berkeley, for others in environmental psychology programs, and operates in the fuzzy overlap of environmental psychology and environmental design. Contrast this approach and publication pattern with the urban ethnologists publishing like the *Journal of Urban Ethnology,* the old *Urban Life.* Do the two groups ever communicate with one another? The fourth approach studies landscape as a mental story (not a map) and internal narrative. Insofar as it has an academic home, that home is in comparative literature, or perhaps American studies.

Almost all workers operate within one of these categories or subcategories. Among the few exceptions, J. B. Jackson comes to mind for his work crossing boundaries between social phenomenon and cultural product; in some ways the work of Anthony King in a different area is similar. Yi-Fu Tuan's unique contribution might be the fact that he works across all four categories, an erudite explorer and taxonomist, a latter-day Humboldt of the landscape experience.

Finally there is the place of internal narrative in the landscape experience. How much of the internal affective impact of a landscape is explainable in structured, fantasy role-playing and how much is immediate and only later elaborated into such? Could this be considered the essence of the landscape experience, the response to which all else is but stimulus? Far too little work is being done in this area. If we must seek a simple, single dichotomy most useful and comprehensive in understanding the landscape experience, it might be the distinction between the external landscape of behavior, social interaction, and political and legal obligation and the internal landscape of fantasy, contemplation, and emotion: the external landscape of social responsibility and the internal landscape of personal gratification.

What has happened to the intense aesthetic landscape experience in all our investigations? Have we no room for that kind of exceptional, "high," landscape experience, by its nature distinct from the ordinary, utilitarian, information-processing landscape experience? No room . . . or maybe no guts to take it on? Can't we begin to try to understand that experience in the terms of modern analytical techniques? An intellectual approach to the landscape that makes no attempt to deal with the power of Ryoan-ji, or Stourhead, or that first view of the Front Range is shamefully incomplete.

It is time to consider the entire range of the landscape experience. We need discussion. We need taxonomy. We need comprehensive frameworks—the plural intentional. This is the age of specialized work, for good as well as for bad, but we need a vision beyond this specialization. This does not mean some grand, unified field cosmology of the landscape experience. If I were granted one wish it would be for a renewal of the eighteenth- and nineteenth-century debate on the nature of the landscape experience, updated with the tools and the vocabulary of the social and behavioral sciences of the twenty-first century.

❧ ❧ ❧ ❧ Garden, Meaning, and Symbols

Can we really revive the art of the garden, that formal and floral sensitivity and technique that finally died in the 1930s? Can we any longer know what our gardens mean, indeed whether they can have meaning? Can we conceive a symbolism to provide that "something else" that gardens are said to mean. Never mind that both modern and postmodern design, from gilded antennas through chrome-plated capitals to regiments of golden frogs, came a cropper on this issue. Take any camp motif, weave around it enough references familiar to readers of the *New York Review of Books* or *Sporting News,* and, presto, a *symbol*! Is it so hard to understand that for a design to succeed as a powerful symbol, it must use symbols that are commonly agreed upon and not just individually selected, symbols that connote affective meaning and not mere intellectual cleverness, symbols that are placed in a context accepted as appropriate? Is it so hard to understand how tough a job that is in a culture as centrifugal and pluralistic as ours? Maybe the time when gardens can mean something else is past and not yet come again. Marc Treib asked, "Must a garden mean?" No, of course not. But when it does, it offers one more level of enrichment to our lives.

⸙ ⸙ ⸙ ⸙ Mystiques and Constructs

Pick up any article on landscape architecture theory today and you have a good chance of encountering the phrase "nature as a cultural construct." But while the phrase is ubiquitous, its ramifications and meanings are seldom discussed. The concept originates in the rejection of the centuries-old idea of nature as a constant, an objective reality "out there," a given. Beyond that, "nature as cultural construct" possesses two distinct meanings relevant to landscape design. One meaning—and stripped temporarily of its usual political baggage—is that different cultures have different views of nature; each culture has its own beliefs, attitudes, perceptions, definitions, and even uses for nature. But at the turn of the second millennium, "nature as a cultural construct" can also refer to the fact that modern science and technology allow us to transform "natural" systems long considered impervious to human manipulation. A profession charged with remaking the landscape, natural and artificial, must understand and address both these meanings, particularly given the cultural and technological developments that will be at our disposal (or us at theirs) over the coming decades.

This concern with the cultural nature of nature rests on a few basic questions. In the words of George Robertson and the other editors of *FutureNatural,* the questions concern

> the construction and reproduction of "nature," "the ways that this "nature" is then instrumental in defining what is or is not natural, and how formulations of "what is natural" eventually attain the status of convention that presents "nature" and the "natural" as seemingly unproblematic. But central to these themes are also questions about the future configurations of "nature" and "the natural" in the light of technological developments that threaten radically to disrupt most of the certainties we hold about the social world.

Before addressing these questions, recall the number and nature of intellectual or semi-intellectual issues that the profession and discipline have been through over the last decades. Do we remember homeostasis, systems theory, bricolage, left brain/right brain, chaos theory, and fractals? How long did those last, why did they die, and more importantly, what, if anything, of use did we learn from them? Shouldn't we be a bit rueful over our flirtations with these issues, or maybe better put, catchphrases? But "nature as cultural construction" is a different animal. In one sense, we have been this way before. The 1970s preoccupation with ecology as the governing paradigm of landscape architecture was also a statement about our relation to the natural world. While we long ago grew out of some of its more flowery rhetoric (remember "if you're not part of the solution, you're part of the problem," or TINSTAAFL, "There is no such thing as a free lunch"), ecology still reigns as a prominent paradigm in our discipline and our profession. Today's "sustainability" and our fascination with "green roofs" are living, useful, long-term results of that four-decades-old paradigm, even for us who wince at the verb "greening."

That ecological mystique and the concept of nature as a cultural construct differ in several ways. The former was a mass social and cultural movement; Stewart Brand's *Whole Earth Catalog* was its seed and manifesto. Landscape architecture grabbed the idea early and became one of its most vocal advocates, its influence waning as corporate and government and longer established university disciplines took over. The latter is a product of a small core of revisionist academics mostly in the humanities. Its influence seldom strays beyond the confines of the graduate seminar. The ecological mystique offered clear directions, even commandments, to designers . . . even if it usually required living with inconsistencies and trade-offs. The idea that nature is a cultural construct has no such clear linkage to or impact on design per se.

Despite these differences, however, the two positions share a basic commonality. *They both are normative statements about the relations of human nature and the nature of nature itself.* In *FutureNatural* Kate Soper, a British philosopher, offers a striking comparative analysis of the two positions.

> While the ecologist refers to a pre-discursive nature which is being wasted and polluted, postmodernist theory directs us to the ways in which relations to the nonhuman world are always historically mediated, and indeed "constructed" through specific conceptions of human identity and difference. Where the focus of the one is on human abuse of an external nature with which we have failed to appreciate our affinities and ties of dependency conduct, the other is targeted on the cultural policing functions of the appeal to "nature" and its oppressive use to legitimize social and sexual hierarchies and norms of human conduct. While the one calls on us to respect nature and the limits it imposes on cultural activity, the other invites us to view the nature-cultural opposition as itself a politically instituted and mutable construct.

To Soper, the protagonists of nature as ecology and nature as cultural construct are, respectively, the Green Party of Germany and the academic acolytes of Michel Foucault and Jean Baudrillard. I do not know how much overlap or exchange exists between these constituencies in Europe. In landscape architecture, in North America, the two factions coexist, easily and comfortably, in the office and classroom, sliding past one another with neither friction nor engagement; this is perhaps not surprising, given the unphilosophical, nonconfrontational, and apolitical character of the profession and discipline on this side of the Atlantic. But we should ask: What roles do these positions play in landscape architecture and how do they also relate (or not) to each other?

It is easier to describe the place of ecological ideas and ideals in landscape architecture, because they date back to the 1950s and '60s, to the days of Stanley White and Ian McHarg. If those who adhere to these ideas have lacked—at least since the early '70s—the passion of the Green Party, they have been guilty of fewer excesses and indulgences. Cultural geographers have argued convincingly that "untouched nature" is a myth and that most of the globe has been significantly altered by human action. Ecology as a scientific inquiry has been supplemented by ecological planning and management based on monitoring change and human intervention in natural systems.

The position of thoughtful landscape architects about nature as a cultural construct is less clear, probably because this idea is newer and offers no easy links to parameters, constraints, and inspirations for design. Unfortunately, so far this notion has mostly been used to demonstrate some would-be theorists' sophistication and currency. "Nature as a cultural construct" is too often associated, in fact, with predictable condemnations of capitalism, commodification, consumerism, objectification, modernity, humanism, the Enlightenment, et cetera.

It is curious that the idea of nature as cultural construct should be a marker of millennial intellectual status, because it is a well-established complex of ideas within the modernist design tradition. More than forty years ago, in my first architectural history course, I listened to Alfred Caldwell condemn the Renaissance and Enlightenment principles of design as a curse upon architecture—a pox that had kept architecture in thrall to a shallow dependence upon style for over four centuries, at least until William Paxton and Louis Sullivan. Clarence Glacken's *Traces on the Rhodian Shore* is more than three decades old now; it dates from the time when geographer Yi-Fu Tuan—sometimes referred to by colleagues as the humanist relict of their discipline—was offering what still remain the most articulate insights into the idea of nature as structured by culture (in a series of papers that preceded his seminal *Topophilia*). Authors as widely respected and diverse as J. B. Jackson and Denis Cosgrove have also explored the concept. But if the idea of the cultural structuring of nature is not new, what is new and important is the recognition of differences between people and perceptions not only across cultures but also within them, and the relation of those differences to power and control.

Two aspects of the use of the phrase "nature as social construction," and of its epistemological and rhetorical underpinnings, are worth remarking upon. First, while underscoring the intellectual dependence of landscape architecture upon other disciplines, it demonstrates a shift—or maybe a drift—in the source of that dependence, from literary theory to cultural studies. Leaving aside the larger dangers of any dependency, this change is to be welcomed, for cultural studies shares with landscape design a concern for the social and cultural aspects of place and space, not to mention "nature," and brings to these subjects a powerful set of tools and the fervor of a burgeoning discipline. Second, the concept has mostly been used to position nature, landscape, and landscape design in relation to the cultural and value systems in which these are embedded and which they serve. If "nature is a cultural construct" is taken as an axiom of landscape theory, then "landscape is a cultural product" is a self-evident corollary.

In fact, this corollary is now producing some of the most interesting and intellectually respectable studies of landscapes and landscape architecture since the eighteenth century, from new looks at the place of the mythic Western landscape in American society to scholarly examinations of the cultural contexts and constraints of specific design periods and practitioners. Unfortunately, this intellectual work deals mostly with what can be termed contextual theory and inquiry, examining how concepts of nature relate to diverse discourses and systems outside the field of landscape design. It needs to be distinguished (but not isolated) from explorations internal to the discipline of landscape architecture about the relationship between theory, design, product, and user. The idea of nature and landscape as cultural products might be a potential link between diverse realms of inquiry, if we ask a few pertinent questions.

First, beyond raising cultural awareness, how might the acceptance of "nature as a cultural construct" influence landscape architects as active interveners in nature? What mandates might it impose? What options might it offer to designers?

Beyond its use in ungrounded and abstract discussion, the concept of nature as a cultural construct is sometimes associated with the idea of "site as palimpsest"; this association has often produced site-specific designs that refer to the different uses, periods, and cultures associated with a particular place. An early example of site-as-palimpsest design is Richard Haag's Gasworks Park in Seattle (although the 1970s beginnings of this work predate the academic popularity of that phrase). More recent designs that make notable use of this theoretical concern are the waterfront reclamation projects of George Hargreaves. And, at least programmatically, the work of Hargreaves and his associates merges nature as ecology and as cultural phenomenon. Whether visitors to these projects comprehend their philosophical intentions is, of course, open to question. And so far the discipline has managed to avoid this kind of question. But I would argue that if we are determined to understand "nature as a cultural construct," then we must make explicit, in our designs and our rhetoric, exactly whose or what cultural construct we have in mind. Are we trapped within the construct of late twentieth-century global capitalism, deploring it as cultural critics but doing its bidding as designers? Or are we designing a construct for the northeastern seaboard–Bay Area–highbrow designer culture? Or, following the critical-regionalist ideas of Kenneth Frampton, do we want our designs to reflect and express locally grounded cultural constructs and in this manner to resist the forces of globalization?

Pursuing these issues could only be to our good, but caution is called for. First, we need to be more sophisticated in our use of the term "culture." It has been some time since anthropologists discarded the traditional view of culture as a monolith and progressed to the idea of cultural expression as the shifting outcome of transactions between competing groups and agencies. The current dependence upon cultural studies, while holding other pitfalls, will probably keep landscape design clean on that score for a time. Second, we must remember that culture works at many levels. The older geographical literature on the American landscape, for instance, assumed an overarching dominant type with only minor regional subthemes. Today, of course, we dispute such thinking. But even within the bounds of a vague and rather permissive national construct of landscape, however, most individual concepts of nature are influenced by the various subcultures that now make up our culture—not only racial, sexual, or ethnic subcultures, but also those complexes of attitudes and behaviors that the anthropologist Amos Rapoport termed "lifestyles." Certainly a good ol' boy duck hunter has a different lifestyle and a different "construction of nature" than does an Audubon Society birdwatcher.

To deal honestly with nature as a cultural construct we must recognize diverse scales of constructs, from the panhuman to the cultural/lifestyle to the individual. Scale here is maybe a dangerous word. Global does not necessarily imply most important. To explore cultural constructs is not necessarily to start with the most "universal" or "basic" level and move "down" through levels of decreasing generality and increasing specificity. The world doesn't work that way; neither does design. Global, cultural, lifestyle, and individual constructs are not discrete, bounded sets, nesting one within another in some usable operational hierarchy; rather they are loose, changing accumulations, intersecting and overlapping, shifting in importance and priority.

So how might we move "nature as a cultural construct" beyond its hermetic intellectual realm? Make it a theory that could indeed inform practice? One obvious way would be to attend to the behavioral and cultural aspects of design in education and disciplinary discourse. Ironically, this would probably entail the return to a curriculum—less formalistic than that in favor today—that includes behavioral aspects of design thought so important in leading design schools fifteen or twenty years ago but now out of fashion.

Nature can be considered a cultural construct not only intellectually but also materially. Contemporary techniques allow us to construct pieces of nature with unprecedented sophistication and power; not only can designers conceptualize any nature we please, now we can in many cases build it. But this new ability can make us hesitant; we approach these potential powers tentatively, perhaps from lack of imagination or perhaps because of scruples that remain from 1970s ecological purism. The actual construction of new versions of nature seems confined in narrow paths, bounded on one edge by Martha Schwartz's use of aggressively human-made materials and on the other by the exhibit *Eco-Revelatory Design: Nature Constructed/Nature Revealed,* which toured the country some time ago. Two very different projects from that exhibition both show physically constructed nature and incorporate clear ideas of cultural construction. In a project in a small city in Minnesota, Joan Iverson Nassauer used the technology associated with street resurfacing and storm water infiltration to reconstruct drainage and biodiversity while respecting the conservative working-class culture of a neighborhood. In a second project, which raises and reflects upon the issues of pollution and political control, Kristina Hill used more sophisticated hydraulic technology in the reclamation of a German landscape that had been profoundly damaged by strip mining.

In general, though, regarding the business of creating nature, landscape design has got a long way to go to match the wizardry of, say, the Walt Disney Company, or of some contemporary nature filmmakers. Disney is the master of the composite landscape, that where the natural and the artificial coexist, exchange roles, even merge. Current cinematic techniques, which condense time, space, and scale, allow us to experience "nature" on film in ways we never could in reality. We could construct, conceptually and physically, experiential composites of the natural and the artificial that would make projects like Martha Schwartz's Whitehead Institute for Biomedical Research look as tame as perennial borders. The techniques of Disney and contemporary filmmakers, as well as those of scientists and engineers, are ours if we want them. Apparently we do not, at least not yet. Landscape architects have mapped out a moral terrain, clear even to the designer of the dullest parking lots; within this terrain, firms that espouse ecological purism, like Andropogon, occupy the high ground, while the manipulators of the real, like Disney, are somewhere near the waste pit. Perhaps landscape architects, unlike philosophers such as Kate Soper, have trouble reconciling "nature as ecology" with "nature as cultural construct" because the design discipline has yet to push the latter to its limits. And until we do, we won't have earned our scorn for the Imagineers.

⩘ ⩘ ⩘ ⩘ The Postmodern Landscape

Our power as a society to ravage, transform, and create landscapes has grown such that many landscapes, landscape experiences, and maybe even our existence are threatened. But, compared to earlier ways of life, most of us have little individual experience in making landscapes or, excepting farmers and hunters, deeply participating in them.

Tourism, in contrast, is the essential condition of postmodern existence. Postmodern life is the triumph of the outsider's landscape over the insider's. While we make few landscapes, while we are seldom insiders, we are daily bombarded with hundreds of images of other landscapes, real and imaginary. We have moved from a telling and hearing society to a writing and reading (and painting and hanging and viewing) society to what? A flash and glimpse culture? My trouble finding words to describe a phenomenon we all experience tells us something about that change. We were quick to adopt Marshall McLuhan's glitziest terms, but we have ignored his observations on the difficulty of separating image, meaning, and medium. The term "global village" has become common coin without our considering that it is producing a global village landscape, one in which images of landscapes we shall never visit are as familiar to us as those of our own village, or city. We might wonder whether the experience of landscape, its role, and its interpretation are changing. Whatever the faults of nineteenth-century landscape painting, it generated a lively and stimulating debate about the nature of the landscape experience, its variety, and its relation to images and symbols. Maybe a contemporary John Ruskin could help us make sense of our contemporary, imagineered, world.

✴ ✴ ✴ ✴ The Goose and the Dish

Is it so bad, then, to be a tourist? I would hope that by now that long-standing and condescending dichotomy between travel and tourism has disappeared. I never did understand why bad water, spoiled food, multitudes of insects, thieving merchants, and smelly, dangerous, overcrowded buses were requirements for an "authentic" landscape experience. One is either an insider or one is not. J. B. Jackson, reflecting back upon decades of teaching, concluded that his purpose had been that of producing intelligent tourists. All right, tourists then. But what kind of landscape will we be experiencing? A very different one, I believe.

A clue can be seen in our own not urban American landscape: a richly productive agriculture overlaid by the homes and proliferating appurtenances of those who see the land primarily as a residential amenity. It is produced not only by residents who have no ties to agriculture but by other new population types and attitudes: high-tech recreation that views nature as only an exciting stage set; agricultural workers who commute, just as city dwellers one time did, miles a day from their residence to work eight hours and are paid with checks from a bank from some remote state on the account of Happimeadows AgriSystems, Inc.

I have noted before the initial impact of the automobile, propane tank, and septic tank. Then came satellite television with its attendant minion VCRs, one more amenity to enjoy without locational restrictions. The

Internet after the turn of the century has been a major shaper of the new landscape, not only allowing more people but enticing creative people, formerly dependent on conventional urban infrastructure and face-to-face meeting. All this is more than a new demography, a new density, and a new habitation settlement and transportation pattern.

The new landscape relies heavily on privatization of services and seems to obey no laws except those of the market place. Nationally franchised dealers handling propane, fertilizer, herbicide, and equipment rental anchor the new landscape. Placement of the human artifacts on the land, even the use of the land, sometimes seems arbitrary. We have a traditional image of what the landscape should look like, an image based on real agriculture landscapes in which use and habitation followed certain patterns. Even if the depth and causes of the patterns and their interacting complexities were not visible or even known by the outsider, there was still a sense that some form of order was operating, that there were coherence and a logic rather than arbitrariness. We make sense of our exterior world by vision, and if there is no apparent visual order to this landscape, how are we to understand it? How are we to feel other than ill at ease in it? The problem is that this new landscape is in large part aspatial.

Our traditional landscape was understood in terms of a sophisticated (if seldom useful) regional science, central place theory, hierarchical settlement, agricultural land rent, highest and best use, and so on. But the new landscape is a *network,* based on different motivations, economics, and sociology. It is a network with many fewer locational, more spatial distance restrictions than the old network and, in fact, with the electronic communications about as aspatial as any phenomena in space could be. We have not developed any theoretical knowledge from this network yet, and such models that come will be vastly different and much more complex, and less spatial even, than those we remember.

How are we to understand the relationship between this new network and the traditional agriculture pattern? It's easy to think of the new landscape as seeping out of the city along the interstates and inundating the weakest cracks in the old landscape, as if it were some spreading disease. Easy, but not useful. If we were to use an epidemiological model, we would better think in terms of a widespread airborne spore dispersion in a time of global travel and transport, for the new landscape seems to land in unexpected spots and form few predictable clusters, tentacles, or centers.

The most useful view of the new landscape is as a very loose net laid down over, but almost independent of, the old landscape. Interaction between the two takes place at infrequent and unpredictable junctures, or nodes or linkages.

This is the best model of globalization of the first century of the new millennia: a vast network of new technologies and communications draped loosely over a world landscape still largely agricultural or extractive. Travelers and anthropologists have noted the concurrent existence of these networks in less developed areas of the world. In the tropical rain forest, for example, a network of river travel based on the outboard engine lies over an older trade network of paths and the occasional road. DVD players dot jungle and desert along the network of electrical transmission lines. In our new American landscape its essential services seem less those of bank and grocery store than beauty parlor and video rental outlet. Few of us have even recognized this new landscape yet, much less begun to understand it. Certainly no scholars, planners, theoreticians, predicted its coming, although Jackson did forecast some of its characteristics: mobility, change, sensory rewards, and transience.

We now inhabit two differently organized landscapes, one overlaid upon the other. Trailer owners change the holiday costumes on the concrete goose that stands in the front yard next to the satellite dish. The major engine driving change is money. Money sees the land and its development as product. This is true, in different guises, in socialist countries and capitalist countries alike. Nowhere is it more blatant than in the developed world. Lenin asked, "Who profits?" The answer is not easy to find; profits are passed through levels upon levels of financing and manipulation and, unlike the millionaires' mansions of past times, are not discernible by simply examining the visible landscape.

By current indications, the landscape ahead of us is unlikely to be of ecological soundness, or of justice, or of equity. How ironic that contemporary design, at least at its high end, celebrates this world. If it lacks the unity of earlier styles, maybe that is for the better, or at least more appropriate for our time. Indeed, that might be the best we can hope for in the near future: patches of beauty, of brilliant splendor, scattered glowing gems over a global landscape of privilege and power, of disorganization and disenfranchisement. Not a landscape of dark, satanic mills amid a green and pleasant land of smallholders, but the crystal and concrete information nodes of Bangalore or Karnataka rising above urban squalor and high-technology agricultural plantations. Earth may abide forever, but not the earth we know.

◢ ◢ ◢ ◢ Closings

The essays in this book have dealt mostly with the character and evolution of the physical landscape, and how people use it and behave in it. I have looked at that landscape more through a cultural or behavioral lens than through a psychological or emotional lens. But once we move behind and beyond the threshold of an adequately functional landscape, beyond issues of moral or ethical values or of visual "quality," we are left to face the more difficult issues of emotion and affect. A focus on the experiential aspects can cross the line into memoirs, surveys, and ultimately bad poetry, but we need to go there. However, a few cautions, observations, and warnings are in order.

Affective response to the landscape is multisensory. That cliché fills gardening books with fragrant flowers, gentle wafting breezes, and the hum of bees. But in fact every encounter with the landscape is multisensory, if only no more than the discomfort of extreme temperatures, the corrosive smell of the bad atmosphere, or the noises that impinge upon that experience.

The once fashionable visual assessment discipline, with its single-sense emphasis on vision, was a major setback for thinking about the landscape. A more dangerous inadequacy was the blatant assumption that a one-off, stationary, and instantaneous experience that ignored not only the nonvisual senses but movement, duration, history, and expectation could tell us anything of value about experiencing a landscape beyond locating photo ops. These obvious limitations are sometimes acknowledged by workers in the area, but dismissed as nonquantitative and anyway irrelevant for the particular case at hand. The extreme of the visual assessment mind-set leads to parody and the art world hoax of Komar and Melamid landscape paintings.

There is still another failure in our attempts to even categorize, much less understand or explain, the landscape experience. Variability is overarching, dominant. Until the last two decades, discussion on the landscape experience was a classic humanistic approach dealing more with power than poverty, with centers rather than margins, and assumed, if not quite universality, a great commonality across all peoples and landscapes. The new landscape scholarship has taken a revisionist approach that, fairly enough, emphasizes the role of cultural dominants, coercion to some, that suppress or marginalize other attitudes and settings. But being both hominid and the member of a particular culture does not exhaust the range of our reaction to the landscape. We also interact with the landscape as unique *individuals* with our own and idiosyncratic gestalts. Here variability becomes the dominant shaper. Erich Isaac observed long ago that the primary relation of people is to other people; peoples' relation to their landscape is secondary. Psychologists tell us, for example, that the need for, or an aversion to, external stimuli will vary with the power one feels over one's surroundings. The very young, the very old, and the very sick seek different stimuli from their surroundings than those in the prime of their age and power and health. Our momentary mind and mood will shape our landscape reaction; sometimes we are just too dull or distracted to react to what is at other times a comforting, pleasurable, or stimulating environment. Finally, is it heresy to acknowledge that there are people to whom the landscape is simply not that important?

Maybe the most common and important shaper of our landscape experience is the social surround within which we experience it. The Kaplans, Mark Francis, and others have pointed out that community gardeners rate social interaction and support as among their most important pleasures, and Francis has used the presence or absence of such interpersonal reaction as being the prime difference between park and garden. I have visited compelling landscapes, sometimes alone, sometimes with friends or colleagues. Neither experience is better, they are simply different. Lastly, for a tourist, or a designer, going to visit a famous setting, expectations are no doubt the dominant factor shaping that initial encounter.

Finally, there is the probability that a memorable landscape experience links the mood and setting of the moment not only with one's own personal history but with a sense of a possible future as well. When we internalize such an experience we construct our own psychic timeline of landscape memory and anticipation. This complex concept of landscape experience has too many implications to treat here, but André Aciman's work is rich in speculations on and explorations of this issue. For some years I taught a landscape course to thirty or forty bright graduate students, most all of them with a good bit of travel experience behind them, as well as a design sensibility. With Aciman's ideas in mind, I asked, "How many of you have found somewhere a landscape that you immediately loved, which gave you a joyous high?" Almost all raised their hands. I then asked them if, at that time, they fantasized a return—with money and a lover. Embarrassed silence, furtive looks, one or two hands hesitantly raised and then almost total assent, a dramatic example of building our own internal landscape timelines.

I now look back over a lifetime of landscape experiences, some as powerful in memory as the first experience, poignant as ever. I remember, long ago, walking the empty streets of Beacon Hill after midnight, neither drunk nor as yet completely sober, realizing that I was walking in a De Chirico landscape. I remember magic: that first nighttime sight of Salt Lake City as I drove over the crest from the east; swimming naked with a lover in a moonlit Mediterranean; watching the rising sun color Ayers Rock a deep vermilion; being mesmerized by the slow, even, spectacular parade of the great Canadian grain elevators across the High Plains of Saskatchewan and Alberta. I remember feeling what I can only call awe at the architectural innovation that has been Barcelona for centuries; and the great kaleidoscopic jumble of centuries, side-by-side, one over another, in Riga and Istanbul.

At a different scale of vision and emotion I remember landscapes seen from the air: flying east to west across the United States, watching the European irregularity of metes and bounds land give way to the mile square grandeur of the Jeffersonian grid, the grid becoming coarser in grain and then disappearing in the arid High Plains of the center of the continent, only to appear again in splendid isolation wherever there was water and agriculture. The broad range of the Rockies, then the flat regularity of California rice lands, and always upon landing the first smell of California air, soft as spring. I recall the northern air route from midcontinent to Europe: the endless sodden lands of Labrador, the greatest expanse of flat, roadless land I have ever seen; icebergs in calving season off southern Greenland (while fending off a Lufthansa Valkyrie trying to lower my blinds for the movie); and late on a clear night, high over Paris, the black thread of the Seine wandering through a sparkling blanket of lights. There are smells, of course; probably everyone has his own madeleine and tea. My earliest lifelong memory, as prosaic as it is powerful, is of a cooking grease-laden blast of air from a restaurant fan when I was not yet four. Decades later I spent my first afternoon in China trying to figure out what was sending me back to my childhood, finally realizing that it was coal smoke, that coal smoke that in my childhood blanketed Chicago on every cold winter night. I carry always the two scents of Colorado's Front Range: dry ponderosa needles in the summer and piñon smoke on that first cold night in autumn.

I remember being alone looking for snuffboxes in the streets of Guangzhou, and Ashanti art in Nairobi. Being alone in the Big Bend country, the best and maybe the only way to experience that landscape. Being alone, feeling alone, half-Hopper, half-kitsch, after midnight in an Arizona diner, feeding Glenn Yarborough songs into a jukebox over and over. Aloneness has been a recurring theme of the great travelers, but I can still feel it . . . now . . . here. It is my own sublime.

Youth looks ahead and yes, the older do look back, but anticipation and memory are dialectic partners in our internal landscapes. Words of Proust and Stegner, the interplay of memory and present, of the transient and the imprinted, resonant to me for so long, now bring even deeper meaning and richer recollection. Thomas Wolfe was wrong. You can go home again, for we have many homes.

READINGS

Abbott, Berenice, and Bonnie Yochelson. 1997. *Changing New York*. New York: The New Press, The Museum of the City of New York, distributed by W. W. Norton.

Abrioux, Yves. 1985. *Ian Hamilton Finlay: A Visual Primer*. Edinburgh: Reaktion Books.

Aciman, André. 2001. *False Papers: Essays on Exile and Memory*. New York: Picador.

Adams, Ansel. 1972. *Ansel Adams: Recollected Moments*. San Francisco: San Francisco Museum of Art.

Adams, Robert. 1981. *Beauty in Photography: Essays in Defense of Traditional Values*. New York: Aperture.

———. 1984. *Why People Photograph: Selected Essays and Reviews*. New York: Aperture.

———. 1985. *To Make It Home: Photographs of the American West*. New York: Aperture.

Adams, Robert, et al. 1975. *New Topographics: Photographs of a Man-Altered Landscape*. Rochester, N.Y.: International Museum of Photography at George Eastman House.

Agee, James. 1957. *A Death in the Family*. New York: Penguin Classics.

Alexie, Sherman. 1993. *The Lone Ranger and Tonto Fistfight in Heaven*. New York: Atlantic Monthly Press.

———. 2000. *The Toughest Indian in the World: Stories*. New York: Atlantic Monthly Press.

Appleton, Jay. 1975. *The Experience of Landscape*. London: Wiley.

Asimov, Isaac. 1954. *Caves of Steel*. New York: Fawcett Crest.

Bachelard, Gaston. 1969. *The Poetics of Space*. Boston: Beacon Press.

Baudelaire, Charles. 1938. "Gardens of the Villa d'Este." *Flowers of Evil*. Translated by Charles and George Dillon and Edna St. Vincent Millay. New York: Harper and Brothers.

Beahan, Virginia, and Laura McPhee. 1998. *No Ordinary Land: Encounters in a Changing Environment*. New York: Aperture.

Blomfield, Reginald, and F. Inigo Thomas. 1892. *The Formal Garden in England*. London: Macmillan.

Blythe, Ronald. 1969. *Akenfield: Portrait of an English Village*. New York: Delta Books.

———. 1979. *The View in Winter: Reflections on Old Age*. New York: Harcourt Brace Jovanovich.

Bradbury, Ray. 1950. *The Martian Chronicles.* Garden City, N.Y.: Doubleday.

Brouws, Jeff. 1997. *Highway: America's Endless Dream.* New York: Stewart, Tabori and Chang.

Byrd, Warren T., Jr. 1986. "Tidal Garden: Eastern Shore of Virginia." *Places* 3 (3): 22–25.

Capek, Karel. 1984. *The Gardener's Year.* Madison: University of Wisconsin Press.

Caponigro, John Paul. 2002. "Making the Visual Verbal." *Communication Arts Magazine* 44 (July): 182–87.

Caponigro, John Paul, and Ken Lassiter. 2001. "John Paul Caponigro: Painting with Photographs." *Photographer's Forum* 23 (February 2001): 10–19.

Caponigro, Paul. 1967. *Paul Caponigro.* New York: Grossman.

———. 1975. *Landscape.* New York: McGraw-Hill.

———. 2002. *New England Days.* Boston: David R. Godine.

Carson, Rachel. 1961. *Death and Life of Great American Cities.* New York: Fawcett Crest.

Castaneda, Carlos. 1971. *The Teachings of Don Juan: A Yaqui Way of Life.* Berkeley: University of California Press.

Cather, Willa. 1927. *Death Comes for the Archbishop.* New York: Alfred A. Knopf.

Caudill, Harry. 1963. *Night Comes to the Cumberlands.* Boston: Little Brown.

Chawla, Louise. 1994. *In the First Country of Places: Nature, Poetry, and Childhood.* Albany: State University of New York Press.

Christenberry, William. 1983. *Southern Photographs.* New York: Aperture.

Church, Thomas. 1955. *Gardens Are for People.* New York: Van Nostrand Reinhold.

Chute, Carolyn. 1985. *The Beans of Egypt, Maine.* New York: Ticknor and Fields.

Clarke, Arthur C. 1962. *Profiles of the Future.* New York: Harper and Row.

Clay, Grady. 1974. *Close-Up: How to Read the American City.* New York: Praeger.

Cobb, Edith. 1959. "The Ecology of Imagination in Childhood." *Daedalus* 88:122–32.

Collins, Peter. 1965. *Changing Ideals in Modern Architecture 1750–1950.* London: Faber.

Davis, Fred. 1977. "Nostalgia, Identity and the Current Nostalgia Wave." *Journal of Popular Culture* 11 (Fall): 414–24.

Davis, Tim. 1991. "Photography and Landscape Studies." *Landscape Journal* 8 (1): 1–12.

Deal, Joe. 1992. *Southern California Photographs 1976–86.* Albuquerque: University of New Mexico Press.

Douglas, Mary. 1970. *Natural Symbols.* New York: Pantheon Books.

Douglas, William O. 1961. "Wilderness and the Molding of American Character." In *Wilderness: America's Living Heritage,* ed. David Brower. San Francisco: Sierra Club.

Duncan, James. 1973. "Landscape Taste as a Symbol of Group Identity." *Geographical Review* 63 (July): 334–55.

Durrell, Lawrence. 1961. *The Alexandria Quartet.* New York: Dutton.

Eckbo, Garrett, Daniel U. Kiley, and James C. Rose. 1939. "Landscape Design: The Urban Environment." *Architectural Record* 85 (May): 70–77.

———. 1939. "Landscape Design: The Rural Environment." *Architectural Record* 85 (August): 68–74.

———. 1940. "Landscape Design in the Primeval Environment." *Architectural Record* 89 (February): 74–77.

Eliade, Mircea. 1959. *The Sacred and the Profane: The Nature of Religion.* New York: Harcourt, Brace.

Erdrich, Louise. 1998. *Antelope Wife.* New York: Harper Perennial.

Fabricant, Carole. 1979. "Binding and Dressing Nature's Loose Tresses: The Ideology of Augustan Landscape Design." In *Studies in Eighteenth Century Culture,* vol. 9, ed. Roseann Runte. Madison: University of Wisconsin Press.

Fairbrother, Nan. 1956. *Men and Gardens.* New York: Alfred A. Knopf.

Fisher, Andrea. 1987. *Let Us Now Praise Famous Women: Women Photographers for the U.S. Government, 1935–1944: Esther Bubley, Marjory Collins, Pauline Ehrlich, Dorothea Lange, Martha McMillan Roberts, Marion Post Wolcott, Ann Rosenor, Louise R. Rosskam.* New York: Pandora Press.

Fitzgerald, F. Scott. 1922. "The Diamond as Big as the Ritz." In *Tales of the Jazz Age.* New York: Vintage.

———. 1963. *The Great Gatsby.* London: Bodley Head.

Francis, Mark. 1985. *The Park and the Garden in the City.* Davis: Center for Design Research, University of California.

Ganzel, Bill. 1984. *Dust Bowl Descent.* Lincoln: University of Nebraska Press.

Giedion, Sigfried. 1967. *Space, Time, and Architecture: The Growth of a New Tradition.* Cambridge, Mass.: Harvard University Press.

Giraud, Deborah D. 1987. "The Meaning of Gardens to Hmong Refugees." In *Meaning in the Garden,* ed. Mark Francis and Randolph T. Hester Jr. Cambridge, Mass.: MIT Press.

Glassie, Henry. 1968. *Pattern in the Material Folk Culture of the Eastern United States.* Philadelphia: University of Pennsylvania Press.

Gohlke, Frank. 1991. *Nuclear Baltimore:* Baltimore: Johns Hopkins University Press.

———. 1992. *Measure of Emptiness: Grain Elevators in the American Landscape.* Baltimore: Johns Hopkins University Press.

———. 1998. *Landscapes from the Middle of the World: Photographs, 1972–1987.* San Francisco: The Friends of Photography.

Gold, Herbert. 1975. "Finding the Times in Offramp City." *New Republic,* 8 February, 11–15.

Graham, David. 1987. *American Beauty.* New York: Aperture.

Guimond, James. 1991. *American Photography and the American Dream.* Chapel Hill: University of North Carolina Press.

Gursky, Andreas. 2001. *Andreas Gursky.* New York: Museum of Modern Art.

Hales, Peter B. 1998. *William Henry Jackson and the Transformation of the American Landscape.* Philadelphia: Temple University Press.

Hall, Edward T. 1966. *The Hidden Dimension.* Garden City, N.Y.: Doubleday.

Hamerton, Philip Gilbert. 1885. *Landscape.* Boston: Robert Brothers.

Hancock, Virgil. 1999. *Open Range and Parking Lots: Photographs of the Southwest.* Albuquerque: University of New Mexico Press.

Hanson, David T. 1997. *Waste Land: Meditations on a Ravaged Landscape.* New York: Aperture.

Harkness, Terence. 1986. "An East Central Illinois Garden: A Regional Garden." *Places* 3 (3): 6–9.

Harrington, Michael. 1962. *The Other America: Poverty in the United States.* New York: Macmillan.

———. 1979. "To the Disney Station: Corporate Socialism in the Magic Kingdom." *Harper's,* January, 35–44.

Harris, Alex. 1993. *Red White Blue and God Bless You: A Portrait of Northern New Mexico.* Albuquerque: University of New Mexico Press.

Healy, Vince. 1987. "The Hospice Garden: The Visitor and the Grieving Process." In *Meaning in the Garden,* ed. Mark Francis and Randolph T. Hester Jr. Cambridge, Mass.: MIT Press.

Hecht, Anthony. 1953. "The Gardens of the Villa d'Este." *Kenyon Review* 15 (2): 208–12.

Helphand, Kenneth. 1985. "The Garden." Paper given at the meeting of the Council of Educators in Landscape Architecture, Urbana, Ill.

Hemingway, Ernest. 1939. "A Clean and Lighted Place." In *The Snows of Kilimanjaro and Other Stories.* New York: Scribner's.

Herbert, Frank. 1965. *Dune.* Philadelphia: Chilton.

Howell, Sandra C. 1989. "Environmental Design: The Pic-Up-Stix of Academia." Unpublished paper circulated at the meeting of the Environmental Design Association, Black Mountain, N.C.

Howett, Catherine. 1987. "Gardens Are Good Places for Dying." In *Meaning in the Garden,* ed. Mark Francis and Randolph T. Hester Jr. Cambridge, Mass.: MIT Press.

Hudson, W. H. 1942. "A Boy's Animism." In *Far Away and Long Ago.* New York: E. P. Dutton.

Isaac, Erich. 1960. "Religion, Landscape and Space." *Landscape* 9 (2): 14–18.

Jackson, J. B. 1957. "The Abstract World of the Hot-Rodder." *Landscape* 7 (2): 22–27.

———. 1980. *The Necessity for Ruins and Other Essays.* Amherst: University of Massachusetts Press.

Jacobs, Jane. 1962. *Silent Spring.* New York: Fawcett Crest.

Jay, Martin. 1993. *Downcast Eyes: The Denigration of Vision in Twentieth-Century French Thought.* Berkeley: University of California Press.

Jenshel, Len. 1992. *Travels in the American West.* Washington, D.C.: Smithsonian Institution Press.

Johnson, Hugh. 1979. *The Principles of Gardening.* New York: Simon and Schuster.

Josephson, Kenneth, and Sylvia Wolf. 1979. *Kenneth Josephson: A Retrospective.* Chicago: The Art Institute of Chicago.

Jussim, Estelle, and Elizabeth Lindquist-Cock. 1985. *Landscape as Photograph.* New Haven: Yale University Press.

Kaplan, Stephen. 1983. "A Model of Person-Environment Compatibility." *Environment and Behavior* 15 (3): 311–32.

Kazin, Alfred. 1958. *A Walker in the City.* New York: Grove Press.

Kingston, Maxine Hong. 1976. *The Woman Warrior: Memoirs of a Girlhood among Ghosts.* New York: Knopf.

Kowinski, William. 1978. "The Malling of America." *New Times,* 1 May, 30–55.

Kroeber, A. L. 1957. *Style and Civilizations.* Ithaca: Cornell University Press.

Kubler, George. 1962. *The Shape of Time: Remarks on the History of Things.* New Haven: Yale University Press.

Ladd, Florence C. 1977. "Comments on . . ." In *Children, Nature, and the Urban Environment.* Upper Darby, Pa.: U.S. Forest Service.

———. 1977. "Residential History: You Can Go Home Again." *Landscape* 21 (2): 15–20.

Lassus, Bernard. 1983. "The Landscape Approach of Bernard Lassus." *Journal of Garden History* 3 (2): 79–107.

Leopold, Aldo. 1964. *A Sand County Almanac.* New York: Oxford University Press.

Lewis, Peirce. 1979. "The Unprecedented City." In *The American Land.* New York: W. W. Norton.

———. 1981. "The Urban Invasion of the Rural Northeast." Unpublished paper. Department of Geography, Pennsylvania State University, State College, Pa.

Lippard, Lucy. 1983. "Feminism and Prehistory." In *Overlay: Contemporary Art and the Art of Prehistory.* New York: Pantheon Books.

Louv, Richard. 1983. *America II.* Boston: Houghton Mifflin.

Lowenthal, David. 1968. "The American Scene." *Geographical Review* 58 (January): 61–68.

———. 1975. "Past Time, Present Place: Landscape and Memory." *Geographical Review* 65 (January): 1–37.

Lynch, Kevin. 1972. *What Time Is This Place?* Cambridge, Mass.: MIT Press.

Macdonald, Kent. 1985. "The Commercial Strip: From Main Street to Television Road." *Landscape* 28 (3).

MacLeish, Archibald. 1985. "Epistle to Be Left in the Earth." In *Collected Poems, 1917–1982.* Boston: Houghton Mifflin.

Marcus, Clare Cooper. 1978. "Remembrance of Landscapes Past." *Landscape* 22 (3): 34–43.

———. 1979. *Environmental Autobiography.* Berkeley: Institute of Urban & Regional Development.

———. 1995. *House as Mirror of Self: Exploring the Deeper Meaning of Home.* Berkeley: Conari Press.

Marshall, Lane. 1979. "Agoramania: The Influence of Nostalgia on the Contemporary American Landscape." Unpublished paper. Department of Landscape Architecture, University of Illinois, Urbana.

Martiniere, Stephan. 2006. *Quantum Dreams: The Art of Stephan Martiniere.* Culver City, Calif.: Design Studio Press.

Marx, Leo. 2000. *The Machine in the Garden.* New York: Oxford University Press.

McMurtry, Larry. 1961. *Horseman, Pass By.* New York: Harper and Brothers.

Meatyard, Ralph Eugene. 1974. *Ralph Eugene Meatyard.* New York: Aperture.

Meinig, D. W. 1979. "Symbolic Landscapes." In *The Interpretation of Ordinary Landscapes,* ed. D. W. Meinig. New York: Oxford University Press.

Meyer, Karl E. 1979. "Love Thy City." *Saturday Review,* 28 April, 16–20.

Meyer, Pedro. 1995. *Truths & Fictions: A Journey from Documentary to Digital Photography.* New York: Aperture.

Meyerowitz, Joel. 1990. *Creating a Sense of Place: Photographs.* Washington, D.C.: Smithsonian Institution Press.

———. 2000. *Joel Meyerowitz.* London: Phaidon.

Misrach, Richard. 1987. *Desert Cantos.* Albuquerque: University of New Mexico Press.

———. 1990. *Bravo 20: The Bombing of the American West.* Baltimore: Johns Hopkins University Press.

Momaday, N. Scott. 1968. *House Made of Dawn.* New York: Harper & Row.

Moore, Charles, Gerald Allen, and Donlyn Lyndon. 1979. *The Place of Houses.* New York: Holt, Rinehart and Winston.

———. 1998. *The Poetics of Gardens.* Cambridge, Mass.: MIT Press.

Moore, Charles, and William Mitchell. 1983. "On Gardens." *Mimar* 8:23–29.

———. 1986. "American Edens." *Places* 3 (3): 60–66.

Morris, Wright. 1946. *The Inhabitants: Text and Photos.* New York: C. Scribner's Sons.

Mukherjee, Bharati. 1975. *Wife.* Boston: Houghton Mifflin.

Naipaul, V. S. 1989. *A Turn in the South.* New York: Knopf.

Nairn, Ian. 1965. *The American Landscape: A Critical View.* New York: Random House.

National Museum of American Art. 1992. *Between Home and Heaven: Contemporary American Landscape Photography.* Essays by Merry A. Foresta, Stephen Jay Gould, and Karal Ann Marley. Washington, D.C.: National Museum of American Art, Smithsonian Institution, in association with the University of New Mexico Press.

Newton, Norman. 1957. *Approach to Design.* Cambridge, Mass.: Addison Wesley.

Nickel, Douglas R. 1999. *Carleton Watkins: The Art of Perception.* San Francisco: San Francisco Museum of Modern Art.

Olin, Laurie. 1986. "Brillig and Contrary Gardens." *Places* 3 (3): 52–55.

Ortega y Gasset, José. 1972. *Meditations on Hunting.* New York: Scribner.

Parks, Gordon. 1994. *Arias in Silence.* Boston: Little, Brown.

Peets, Elbert. 1927. "The Landscape Priesthood." *American Mercury* 10 (37): 94–100.

Peterson, R. A., and P. DiMaggio. 1979. "From Region to Class, the Changing Locus of Country Music: A Test of the Massification Hypothesis." *Social Forces* 53 (March): 497–505.

Pfahl, John. 1981. *Altered Landscapes: The Photographs of John Pfahl.* Carmel, Calif.: The Friends of Photography.

———. 1987. *Picture Windows: Photographs by John Pfahl.* Boston: Little, Brown.

————. 1990. *A Distanced Land: The Photographs of John Pfahl.* Albuquerque: University of New Mexico Press.

Plowden, David. 1972. *The Floor of the Sky: The Great Plains.* San Francisco: Sierra Club.

Porter, Eliot. 1963. *The Place No One Knew: Glen Canyon on the Colorado.* San Francisco: Sierra Club.

Powell, Anthony. 1995. *The Kindly Ones,* book 6 of *A Dance to the Music of Time.* Reprint, Chicago: University of Chicago Press.

Pregill, Philip, and Nancy Volkman. 1993. *Landscapes in History: Design and Planning in the Western Tradition.* Hoboken, N.J.: Wiley.

Raphael, Ray. 1985. *Cash Crop: An American Dream.* Mendocino, Calif.: Ridge Times Press.

Rapoport, Amos. 1982. *The Meaning of the Built Environment: A Nonverbal Communication Approach.* Beverly Hills, Calif.: Sage Publications.

Rasmussen, Steen Eiler. 1962. *Experiencing Architecture.* Translated by Eve Wendt. Boston: MIT Press.

Raup, Hugh M. 1966. "The View from John Sanderson's Farm: A Perspective for the Use of the Land." *Forest History* 10 (April): 2–11.

Relph, E. C. 1976. *Place and Placelessness.* London: Pion.

Riley, Robert B. 1980. "Speculations on the New American Landscapes." *Landscape* 24 (3): 1–9.

————. 1987. "Flowers, Power and Sex: Themes in the Literature of Garden Meaning." In *Meaning in the Garden,* ed. Mark Francis and Randolph T. Hester Jr. Cambridge, Mass.: MIT Press.

Robertson, George, et al., eds. 1996. *FutureNatural: Nature/Science/Culture.* New York: Routledge.

Robinson, Kim Stanley. 1993. *Red Mars.* New York: Bantam Books.

————. 1994. *Green Mars.* New York: Bantam Books.

————. 1996. *Blue Mars.* New York: Bantam Books.

Rose, James. 1938. "Freedom in the Garden." *Pencil Points* 19 (October): 640–44.

————. 1939. "Articulate Form in Landscape Design." *Pencil Points* 20 (February): 98–100.

————. 1939. "Why Not Try Science?" *Pencil Points* 20 (December): 777–79.

————. 1958. *Creative Gardens.* New York: Van Nostrand Reinhold.

Rykwert, Joseph. 1972. *On Adam's Hut in Paradise.* New York: Museum of Modern Art Press.

Sassoon, Siegfried. 1949. "Villa d'Este Gardens." In *Collected Poems.* New York: Viking Press.

Scourse, Nicolette. 1983. *The Victorians and Their Flowers.* Portland, Ore.: Timber Press.

Second View: The Rephotographic Survey Project. 1984. By Mark Klett, Ellen Manchester, JoAnn Verburg, Gordon Bushaw, Rick Dingus, and Paul Berger. Albuquerque: University of New Mexico Press.

Shepard, Paul. 1959. "A Theory of the Value of Hunting." In *Transactions of the*

Twenty-Fourth North American Wildlife Conference. Washington, D.C.: Wildlife Management Institute.

———. 1973. *The Tender Carnivore and the Sacred Game.* New York: Charles Scribner.

Shepherd, Jean. 1966. "Harry Gertz and the Forty-Seven Crappies." *In God We Trust, All Others Pay Cash.* New York: Random House, Broadway Books.

Sherman, Cindy. 1990. *Untitled Film Stills.* New York: Rizzoli.

Shore, Stephen. 1982. *Uncommon Places: Photographs.* Millerton, N.Y.: Aperture.

Silko, Leslie Marmon. 1986. "Landscape, History, and the Pueblo Imagination." *Antaeus* 57.

Simak, Clifford. 1971. *City.* London: Sphere.

Sitwell, George. 1909. *On the Making of Gardens.* New York: Charles Scribner.

Smith, Page. 1966. *As a City upon a Hill: The Town in American History.* New York: Knopf.

Solomon, Barbara Stauffacher. 1982. "Green Architecture: Notes on the Common Ground." *Design Quarterly* 120.

Soper, Kate. 1966. "NATURE/'Nature.'" In *FutureNatural: Nature/Science/Culture,* ed. George Robertson, et al. New York: Routledge.

———. 1996. "The Production of Nature." In *FutureNatural: Nature/Science/Culture,* ed. George Robertson, et al. New York: Routledge.

Sopher, David E. 1979. "The Landscape of Home: Myth, Experience, Social Meaning." In *The Interpretation of Ordinary Landscapes,* ed. D. W. Meinig. New York: Oxford University Press.

Sparth, Lou Anders. 2008. *Structura: The Art of Sparth.* Culver City, Calif.: Design Studio Press.

Spreiregen, Paul. 1965. *Urban Design: The Architecture of Towns and Cities.* New York: McGraw Hill.

Starr, Roger. 1966. *The Living End: The City and Its Critics.* New York: Coward McMann.

Stegner, Wallace. 1962. *Wolf Willow.* New York: Viking Press.

Sternfeld, Joel. 1992. *American Prospects: Photographs.* San Francisco: Chronicle Books.

———. 2001. *Stranger Passing.* Boston: Bulfinch.

Stewart, George Rippey. 1953. *U.S. 40: Cross Section of the United States of America.* Boston: Houghton Mifflin.

———. 1954. *American Ways of Life.* Garden City, N.Y.: Doubleday.

Streatfield, David. 1970. "The Tyranny of the Garden." *Landscape Architecture* 60 (January): 96–100.

Sulzinger, Richard. 1979. "Will There Be Any Truck Stops in Heaven? Images of the Landscape in Country and Western Music." Unpublished paper. Department of Landscape Architecture, University of Illinois, Urbana.

Summerson, John. 1963. "The Mischievous Analogy." In *Heavenly Mansions and Other Essays on Architecture.* New York: Norton.

Sun, Xiao Xiang. 1987. "Chinese Gardens." Paper presented at the Department of Landscape Architecture, University of Illinois, Urbana.

Thall, Bob. 1994. *The Perfect City*. Baltimore: Johns Hopkins University Press.

———. 1999. *The New American Village*. Baltimore: Johns Hopkins University Press.

Treib, Marc. 1979. "Traces upon the Land." *Architectural Association Quarterly* 11 (4).

———. 1995. "Must Landscapes Mean?: Approaches to Significance in Recent Landscape Architecture." *Landscape Journal* 14 (Spring): 42–62.

Trillin, Calvin. 1977. "Thoughts Brought On by Prolonged Exposure to Exposed Brick." *New Yorker*, 16 May, 101–7.

Tuan, Yi-Fu. 1974. *Topophilia: A Study of Environmental Perception, Attitudes, and Values*. Englewood Cliffs, N.J.: Prentice-Hall.

———. 1977. "Experience and Appreciation." In *Children, Nature, and the Urban Environment*. Upper Darby, Pa.: U.S. Forest Service.

———. 1977. *Space and Place: The Perspective of Experience*. Minneapolis: University of Minnesota Press.

———. 1984. *Dominance and Affection: The Making of Pets*. New Haven: Yale University Press.

Uelsmann, Jerry N. 1992. *Jerry Uelsmann: Photo Synthesis*. Gainesville: University Press of Florida.

Updike, John. 1987. "The City." In *Trust Me: Short Stories*. New York: Knopf.

Uzzle, Burk. 1973. *Landscapes/Photographs*. Rochester, N.Y.: Magnum Photos/Light Impressions.

———. 1984. *All American*. St. David's, Pa.: St. David's Books.

Vale, Thomas R., and Geraldine R. Vale. 1983. *U.S. 40 Today: Thirty Years of Landscape*. Madison: University of Wisconsin Press.

Varnedoe, Kirk. 1988. *Northern Light: Nordic Art at the Turn of the Century*. New Haven: Yale University Press.

Venturi, Robert, Denise Scott Brown, and Steven Izenour. 1972. *Learning from Las Vegas*. Cambridge, Mass.: MIT Press.

Vergara, Camilo José. 1995. *The New American Ghetto*. New Brunswick: Rutgers University Press.

———. 1999. *American Ruins*. New York: Monacelli Press.

Warner, Sam Bass, Jr. 1987. *To Dwell Is to Garden: A History of Boston's Community Gardens*. Boston: Northeastern University Press.

Watts, May Theilgaard. 1975. "The Fashionable House." In *Reading the Landscape of America*. New York: Macmillan.

Wells, H. G. 1914. *When the Sleeper Wakes*. London: Macmillan.

Westerbeck, Colin, and Joel Meyerowitz. 1994. *Bystander: A History of Street Photography*. Boston: Little, Brown.

White, Minor. 1969. *Mirrors, Messages, Manifestations*. New York: Aperture.

White, Morton and Lucia. 1964. *The Intellectual versus the City*. New York: Signet.

Williams, Robert. 1987. "Rural Economy and the Antique in the English Landscape Garden." *Journal of Garden History* 7 (1): 73–96.

Winningham, Geoff, and Al Reinert. 1986. *A Place of Dreams: Houston, an American City*. Houston: Rice University Press.

Wohlwill, Joachim. 1983. "The Concept of Nature: A Psychologist's View." In *Human Behavior and Environment,* ed. Irwin Altman and Joachim Wohlwill, vol. 6. New York: Plenum Press.

Woiwode, Larry. 1975. *Beyond the Bedroom Wall: A Family Album.* New York: Farrar, Straus, Giroux.

Zelinsky, Wilber. *The Cultural Geography of the United States.* Upper Saddle River, N.J.: Prentice Hall.